OAE

School Counselor Practice Questions

Mometrix

TEST PREPARATION

DEAR FUTURE EXAM SUCCESS STORY

First of all, **THANK YOU** for purchasing Mometrix study materials!

Second, congratulations! You are one of the few determined test-takers who are committed to doing whatever it takes to excel on your exam. **You have come to the right place.** We developed these practice tests with one goal in mind: to deliver you the best possible approximation of the questions you will see on test day.

Standardized testing is one of the biggest obstacles on your road to success, which only increases the importance of doing well in the high-pressure, high-stakes environment of test day. Your results on this test could have a significant impact on your future, and these practice tests will give you the repetitions you need to build your familiarity and confidence with the test content and format to help you achieve your full potential on test day.

Your success is our success

We would love to hear from you! If you would like to share the story of your exam success or if you have any questions or comments in regard to our products, please contact us at **800-673-8175** or **support@mometrix.com**.

Thanks again for your business and we wish you continued success!

Sincerely,
The Mometrix Test Preparation Team

TABLE OF CONTENTS

Practice Test #1

1. A school counselor is tracking graduation rates over the course of several years to determine if a program created to increase the four-year graduation rate is creating the desired result. In analyzing the data, the school counselor is specifically examining which of the following?

a. Trend
b. Mean
c. Mode
d. Standard deviation

2. Mr. Allen is a middle school counselor who has noticed some concerning things with a new student in his school. The student is frequently absent, and when he is in school, he doesn't seem to have clean clothes or school supplies. Mr. Allen is unsure of the cause for these circumstances, but then the student confides in Mr. Allen that he wasn't allowed to eat all weekend as a consequence for a poor grade in school. Mr. Allen is unsure if the child is being abused but is suspicious. What would be the correct course of action for Mr. Allen?

a. Call the student's parents in for a conference to discuss his concerns
b. Ask the teachers if they have noticed anything out of the ordinary about the child
c. Make a report of suspected abuse to Child Protective Services
d. Interview the child to gather more information before making a report

3. A school counselor is evaluating the impact of a behavioral intervention. Which of the following represents outcome data related to disciplinary records?

a. Student surveys about behavior and discipline completed after the intervention
b. Teacher descriptions of behavior on disciplinary referrals submitted after the intervention
c. The number of disciplinary referrals submitted after the intervention
d. Student pre- and post-tests focused on skills learned during the intervention

4. Kesha is a first-year elementary school counselor who is beginning to experience stress and burnout from the many demands of her new role. Which of the following is an appropriate strategy to help Kesha cope with her job stress?

a. Don't check email during the day; instead, save it for at home while on the couch
b. Plan for 10 minutes of quiet meditation in her office after lunch each day
c. Ask her principal to eliminate her afternoon fair-share duty, as she is too busy for it
d. Cancel classroom guidance sessions for a week to get caught up on paperwork

Refer to the following for question 5:

A middle school counselor analyzes attendance data and finds that, in a specific classroom, all but six students have attendance rates above 90%. These six students are failing several classes, mostly due to incomplete assignments, missing homework, and late projects. The teacher has contacted the students' parents but has not tried anything else to address these problems.

5. Which counseling strategy would be most appropriate for the counselor to use in improving attendance in this classroom?

a. Individual counseling sessions with each of the six students with attendance rates below 90%
b. Small group counseling sessions with the six students with attendance rates below 90%
c. Proactive classroom guidance lessons with the entire class focused on school attendance
d. Consultation with the classroom teacher to provide information about the importance of attendance

6. Which of the following is NOT an ASCA Mindsets & Behaviors for Student Success domain?

a. Career
b. Academic
c. Social/emotional
d. College readiness

7. Which of the following examples of group counseling is a primary prevention group?

a. Social skills group
b. Anger management group
c. Alcohol rehabilitation group
d. Eating disorder group

8. Anna is a 7th-grade student whose family has been experiencing a great number of changes, including divorce and relocation. Mr. Hyde, Anna's school counselor, has been working with Anna for several months in individual counseling to address her feelings and experiences. In reflecting on his most recent session with Anna, Mr. Hyde realizes that while Anna has made a great deal of progress in developing coping skills, she is still struggling with anxiety and emotional distress that impacts her daily functioning. What would be the most appropriate next step for Mr. Hyde?

a. Seek additional training and professional development in addressing anxiety so that he can better help Anna with her concerns.
b. Schedule additional individual counseling sessions with Anna to continue to address her needs.
c. Call Anna's parents to discuss Anna's need for continued counseling and suggest a referral for mental health counseling.
d. Work toward the termination of individual counseling sessions and transition Anna to a small group focused on anxiety.

9. In reviewing student outcome data, a school counselor notes that the overall attendance rate of 7th-grade students is much lower than that of 6th- or 8th-grade students. Which of the following is a possible intervention the school counselor could implement based on this piece of data?

a. Surveying 7th-grade students to learn about their feelings about school
b. Initiating a small group focused on improving school attendance
c. Planning classroom guidance for 7th graders focused on improving school attendance
d. Organizing an advisory council to solicit stakeholder feedback on school attendance

10. A school counselor is meeting with the parent of a student in order to discuss the parent's concerns about their child's academic progress. The parent is unsure of how to interpret their child's standardized test results from the state's end-of-grade, norm-referenced tests. Which of the following explanations of the child's test results is accurate for this type of test?

a. "Your child's percentile score compares their performance to their same-age peers across the state."
b. "Your child's percentile score indicates the number of test questions they answered correctly."
c. "Your child's percentile score indicates the percentage of grade-level standards they mastered this year."
d. "Your child's percentile score indicates their potential for success in the next grade level."

11. A school counselor is conducting a small group focused on developing social skills. During a group session, a student begins discussing the misbehaviors of another classmate who is not in the group, making many comments about the student's lack of social skills. Which technique would be appropriate to use in response to these comments?

a. Clarification
b. Blocking
c. Linking
d. Active listening

12. Which of the following statements about the potential impact of sexual orientation on student outcomes is NOT true?

a. Students who identify as LGBTQ are more likely to have low grades than their heterosexual peers.
b. Students who identify as LGBTQ are more likely to have higher rates of truancy than their heterosexual peers.
c. Students who identify as LGBTQ are more likely to report concerns about their safety while at school than their heterosexual peers.
d. Students who identify as LGBTQ do not have significant differences in academic outcomes compared to their heterosexual peers.

13. Which of the following types of data would be best utilized to identify areas for program improvement in an annual school counseling program evaluation?

a. Closing-the-gap action plan results
b. School data profile
c. IQ testing results
d. Program outcome data

14. Which of the following resources would best be used to help a school counselor complete the use-of-time assessment?

a. The school district's student information system
b. Data collected from an online survey
c. A digital calendar, such as Google Calendar
d. Documentation of the counselor's sick leave

15. Which of the following examples represents an appropriate external referral that a school counselor might make?

a. A counselor refers a child with chronic absenteeism due to illness to the school nurse for assistance in developing a health plan.
b. A counselor refers a child with persistent academic difficulties to the school's intervention team for evaluation and support.
c. A counselor refers a child who expresses suicidal ideation to the school psychologist for evaluation of suicide risk.
d. A counselor refers a child who is struggling with significant anxiety for an entire school year for mental health counseling.

16. A counselor is leading an assertiveness training group based on cognitive behavioral therapy. Which of the following techniques would most likely be used in this specific type of group?

a. Role-playing
b. Linking and encouraging
c. Unstructured techniques
d. Empty chair

17. A school counselor conducted a small group focused on improving school attendance. In evaluating the effectiveness of the small group, which of the following types of data would be considered outcome data?

a. Meeting logs outlining student attendance at each small group meeting
b. The average daily attendance rate for participants at the conclusion of the group
c. Student post-tests from the conclusion of each group meeting
d. Student self-evaluations completed at the conclusion of the group

18. Which of the following tests taken by students is an example of an aptitude test?

a. ASVAB
b. End-of-grade test
c. SAT
d. TOEFL

19. An elementary school counselor is conducting a small group focused on managing anger. In a session of the group, the counselor has students create a list of several strategies for dealing with anger and practice role-playing each one. During which stage of the small group process would this activity be most appropriate?

a. Initial/forming stage
b. Transition/storming stage
c. Working/norming stage
d. Termination/adjourning stage

20. When making referrals to community mental health agencies, which of the following procedures is most appropriate?

a. Counselors utilize an emergency mental health provider to screen students and make referrals.
b. Counselors provide families with a pre-approved list of agency referrals provided by the school or district.
c. Counselors provide families with the names of agencies utilized by other students in the school.
d. Counselors avoid making mental health agency referrals and provide individual counseling instead.

21. A school counselor has been assigned to serve on their school's multi-tiered system of support (MTSS) committee. According to the ASCA National Model, which of the following duties would NOT be appropriate for the counselor to undertake as part of this committee?

a. Collaborating with the committee to design and implement intervention plans
b. Evaluating school-wide academic data to help identify students at risk
c. Coordinating individual student intervention plans school-wide
d. Providing proactive, standards-based guidance curriculum to all students

22. Mrs. Lewis is a 3rd-year elementary school counselor whose new building principal has asked her to coordinate the school's end-of-grade testing process. Mrs. Lewis knows that this is an inappropriate activity for school counselors according to the ASCA National Model. Which tools from the ASCA National Model could Mrs. Lewis utilize to advocate for appropriate duties with her principal?

a. The ASCA School Counselor Competencies and ASCA Ethical Standards for School Counselors
b. The counseling program's mission and vision statements
c. Use-of-time assessment and annual agreement
d. School counselor competency and school counseling program assessments

23. Ms. Clark is a counselor who is working with a group of 9th-grade girls experiencing bullying. The four girls used to be friends, but for the last few months, three of the girls have been purposely leaving the fourth girl, Melissa, out of activities, including weekend parties and group work in class. They have also been spreading rumors about Melissa and telling other students not to be friends with her. Which type of bullying is taking place in this scenario?

a. Social bullying
b. Verbal bullying
c. Physical bullying
d. Cyberbullying

24. A school counselor presents data about their school counseling program to their principal. Which of the following would the counselor be most likely to advocate for using process data from the previous school year to support their requests?

a. An appropriate counselor-to-student ratio in accordance with ASCA recommendations
b. Additional professional development about working with students with anxiety
c. The reassignment of inappropriate duties to other professionals within the school
d. Time during the year to train teachers and other staff on student mental health

25. Mrs. Simon is in her second session of individual counseling with a student who wishes to improve her grades. In their first session, the student identified her goal as completing her homework each night and turning it in each day without skipping any assignments; previously, the student had a very poor homework completion rate. Based on solution-focused brief counseling theory, which of the following would Mrs. Simon use to begin their second session?

a. Asking the student what challenges she faced in meeting her goal over the last week
b. Asking the student what is going better since they met last week
c. Asking the student what she was thinking as she completed her homework each night
d. Printing off the student's online grade book and highlighting missing assignments

26. At which stage of the group counseling process does the counselor begin to prepare group members for the termination stage of the group?

a. Selection/screening
b. Initial/forming
c. Transition/storming
d. Working/norming

27. What is the most appropriate group size for an elementary counseling group?

a. Fewer than four students
b. At least four, but no more than six students
c. At least eight, but fewer than ten students
d. Ten students

Refer to the following for question 28:

> Mrs. Tucker, a high school counselor, is evaluating various drug and alcohol prevention curricula for use in her classroom guidance lessons. As a part of this, she is planning a parent information night about drug and alcohol prevention. She is beginning her session with information about risk and protective factors for student drug use.

28. An effective, evidence-based program would be likely to include all of the following EXCEPT:

a. Student pledges or contracts to refrain from drug/alcohol use
b. Factual education about the risks and effects of drug/alcohol use
c. Strategies and skills for stress management
d. Focus on boosting protective factors

29. Which component of a comprehensive school counseling program systematically provides a developmentally appropriate curriculum to all students?

a. Group counseling
b. Classroom guidance
c. Individual counseling
d. Individual student planning

30. Which of the following school counselor activities does NOT take place within the Manage component of the ASCA National Model?

a. Completing a use-of-time assessment
b. Analyzing a results report
c. Creating a closing-the-gap action plan
d. Writing a mission and vision statement

31. Adam is a fourth-grade student whose grades have been low for several months. His teacher reports that he seems to have a hard time grasping the content being taught in class and has foundational gaps in content knowledge. The school's intervention team convenes an initial meeting to discuss a plan of intervention for Adam. Which of the following would be the LEAST appropriate stakeholder to invite to this meeting?

a. Adam's parents
b. The classroom teacher
c. The school psychologist
d. The school counselor

32. Counselors leading groups are ethically obligated to inform participants of the limits of confidentiality in a group setting. At which stage of the group counseling process should this disclosure take place?

a. Selection/screening
b. Initial/forming
c. Transition/storming
d. Working/norming

33. Mrs. Kim is planning to conduct a social skills group for students who demonstrate difficulty with peer interactions and aggressive behavior. She begins her group selection process by asking teachers to identify which students they feel would benefit from the group. What would be the next step in the group selection process?

a. Conduct a brief individual interview with each of the students to determine if they have the social skills to participate in the group effectively.
b. Ask the identified students what they would like to achieve as part of their group participation.
c. Send home permission slips to the parents of the identified students to gain parental consent for group participation.
d. Conduct an individual counseling session with each of the identified students to practice the skills needed to participate in the group.

34. Which of the following group counseling techniques can be used by a counselor to point out commonalities between group members, and thus improve group cohesion and interaction?

a. Clarification
b. Blocking
c. Linking
d. Active listening

35. A new school counselor is working with his administrator to finalize the comprehensive school counseling program for the upcoming school year. The administrator has asked him to identify the components of the counseling program in terms of tiered interventions. Which of the following activities would best fit tier I of a tiered intervention model?

a. Classroom guidance curriculum
b. Small group counseling
c. Individual counseling
d. Closing-the-gap action plan

36. Which of the following is NOT a type of results report utilized by school counselors to evaluate the effectiveness of counseling programs?

a. Curriculum results report
b. Individual counseling results report
c. Small group results report
d. Closing-the-gap results report

37. A school counselor uses an online survey platform to conduct a needs assessment. She receives responses from students, staff, and parents and then uses the data to design programming for the upcoming school year. This use of technology supports which of the following components of the comprehensive school counseling program?

a. Foundation
b. Management
c. Delivery
d. Accountability

38. Marcus is a high school student whose grades have been dropping significantly. He confides in his counselor that he ran away from his parents' home due to his difficult relationship with his stepfather; he has been "couch surfing" with friends for the last several months. Which of the following would be the appropriate first step for Marcus's counselor in responding to this situation?

a. Refer Marcus's case to the school's McKinney-Vento liaison.
b. Report Marcus's runaway status to the police so they can take him home.
c. Discuss Marcus's situation with his teachers to get academic support.
d. Call Marcus's parents to discuss a plan to get him back home.

39. Which of the following would be considered an educational group?

a. A group focused on processing grief and loss.
b. A group focused on teaching parenting skills.
c. A group focused on planning a school event.
d. A group focused on overcoming test anxiety.

40. Which of the following is a primary resource for research on school counselor effectiveness?

a. State school counselor associations
b. University counselor education programs
c. ASCA
d. US Department of Education

41. A high school counselor has a scheduled grade-level meeting with seniors. Which of the following topics would be most appropriate for this meeting format?

a. Study skills and improving grades
b. Upcoming dates and deadlines for college applications and graduation
c. Dating violence prevention
d. NCAA eligibility requirements

42. Which of the following correctly describes the concept of validity as it relates to standardized tests?

a. A valid test score accurately reflects the number of questions answered correctly.
b. If a test is reliable, it is almost always valid.
c. If a test is valid, then it measures what it was intended to measure.
d. A valid test is one that is approved to fulfill federal testing requirements.

43. Sarah is a 4th-grade student who, for the past seven months, has demonstrated restlessness and an inability to focus at school. She is frequently irritable and snaps at her classmates, which has resulted in difficulty maintaining friendships. She complains of frequent headaches and stomachaches and often seems tired. Sarah's mother shared with the school counselor that Sarah has difficulty sleeping at night due to constant worries, and there is no known medical cause for her headaches or stomachaches. Which of the following disorders could Sarah's symptoms be consistent with?

a. Generalized anxiety disorder
b. Autism spectrum disorder
c. Oppositional defiant disorder
d. Attention-deficit hyperactivity disorder

44. Mr. Garner is a school counselor who was asked to participate in an IEP meeting for one of his students. Which of the following best describes the role most appropriate for Mr. Garner in the IEP development process?

a. Mr. Garner should assess the student for special education eligibility and provide data regarding his assessments to the team.
b. Mr. Garner should determine if the child qualifies for an IEP under IDEA and, if so, which category the child qualifies under.
c. Mr. Garner should not participate in the IEP meeting because it is an inappropriate role for a school counselor.
d. Mr. Garner should advocate for the needs of his student and collaborate with the team to ensure the plan is appropriate.

45. A middle school counselor receives a phone call from a case manager at a community agency. The agency provides tutoring and enrichment opportunities for low-income students, and the case manager tells the counselor that they are working with several students at the counselor's school and would like to know how they are progressing academically as a result of their tutoring. Which of the following would be the most appropriate way for the school counselor to work with this agency?

a. Tell the case manager that they will have to ask the students' parents for this information, as FERPA prohibits the counselor from sharing academic information with an outside agency.
b. Provide the students' parents with a release of information form which, once signed, will permit the counselor and case manager to share certain information with each other.
c. Share basic information with the case manager as asked because they represent a stakeholder with a "legitimate educational interest" in the students.
d. Send printed copies of the information with the students to provide to the agency so that they can decide what they would like to share.

46. A school counselor is completing a curriculum results report to evaluate the effectiveness of their classroom guidance program. Which of the following does NOT correctly describe a type of data the counselor would utilize in completing this evaluation?

a. Process data describing the number of classroom guidance lessons completed and the dates of each lesson
b. Perception data collected through feedback surveys after classroom guidance lessons
c. Outcome data describing the number of students who completed each classroom guidance lesson
d. Outcome data describing the improvement in academic achievement as a result of classroom guidance lessons

47. Ms. Meadows is a school counselor in a virtual high school. Which of the following is true of the ethical standards she must follow in a virtual school environment?

a. There is a separate set of ASCA Ethical Standards for online/virtual schooling that Ms. Meadows should follow.
b. There is not an expectation of confidentiality in an online environment due to the nature of virtual schooling.
c. Ms. Meadows needs to ensure she is always reachable in case of an emergency during school hours.
d. Ms. Meadows should educate her students on the effective use of communication technology and appropriate boundaries.

48. Which of the following is NOT true about most commonly used intelligence tests, such as the Stanford-Binet or Wechsler?

a. Intelligence test scores are measured based on a standard bell curve.
b. The average intelligence score is 100, based on the individual's age group.
c. Intelligence tests are statistically valid and reliable.
d. Intelligence tests are valid across different cultures.

49. In a successfully implemented ASCA National Model program, how much of a counselor's time should be dedicated to the Delivery component?

a. 20%
b. 40%
c. 60%
d. 80%

50. During a group counseling session, two group members dominate the conversation, continually "one-upping" each other and appearing to fight for the attention of the group. Which stage of group counseling is the group most likely in while this behavior is occurring?

a. Initial/forming
b. Transition/storming
c. Working/norming
d. Termination/adjourning

51. Which of the following ASCA National Model documents is used to identify and communicate school counseling program priorities to all stakeholders?

a. Annual calendar
b. Annual agreement
c. School data profile
d. Curriculum action plan

52. Which of the following program evaluation activities could NOT be conducted using data pulled from a school's student information system (SIS)?

a. Evaluate individual attendance data after completion of a small group focused on improving attendance.
b. Evaluate enrollment in advanced coursework by student subgroup as part of a closing-the-gap action plan.
c. Evaluate process data regarding the number of parents who participated in an informational meeting.
d. Evaluate discipline outcome data for a group of students who completed an anger management group.

53. According to ASCA, which of the following is an appropriate use of standardized testing results?

a. Using standardized test scores to determine students' eligibility to enroll in advanced coursework
b. Disaggregating standardized test scores to guide programming and instructional decisions
c. Basing promotion and retention decisions on standardized test scores
d. Determining a student's eligibility for Section 504 services based on their standardized test scores

54. In which of the following scenarios might a personality assessment, such as the Myers-Briggs Type Indicator (MBTI), be an appropriate tool?

a. Determining placement in honors coursework
b. Evaluating students for special education services
c. Identifying careers that may be of interest
d. Diagnosing an individual with a personality disorder

55. Which of the following is NOT true about mentor-mentee programs for students?

a. Mentor-mentee programs have a positive impact on student academic achievement.
b. Mentor-mentee programs are a tier I intervention for students at risk.
c. Mentor-mentee programs require parent permission for students to participate.
d. Mentor-mentee programs have a positive impact on the number of disciplinary referrals.

56. A middle school counselor is planning classroom guidance lessons about career options. Which of the following would be the best use of technology in order to increase student knowledge of various careers?

a. Using a survey platform to gather pre-lesson data about careers that interest students
b. Having students utilize a search engine to research a career of interest
c. Having students create a presentation about a career of interest
d. Using a career search such as O*NET to connect careers to skills and interests

57. Based on the ASCA Ethical Standards for School Counselors, which of the following circumstances represents an inappropriate dual relationship that should be avoided?

a. A school counselor counsels a student as well as their older siblings.
b. A school counselor counsels a student who is in a school club sponsored by the counselor.
c. A school counselor counsels a student who is also in a course taught and graded by the counselor.
d. A school counselor counsels a student whose parent works at the school.

58. A school counselor is working as part of a team to evaluate a student for possible learning disabilities. Which of the following methods of data collection would be LEAST appropriate for gathering background information to support the team in selecting appropriate assessments and evaluating the student?

a. Collecting intervention data
b. Reviewing academic records
c. Surveying the student
d. Gathering a health history

59. Which of the following statements about English language learners (ELLs) is NOT true?

a. Typically, ELLs lag behind their English proficient peers in reading.
b. ELL students are not eligible for special education services with an IEP.
c. Spanish is the most common home language for ELLs nationwide.
d. Urban schools typically have a higher percentage of ELLs than suburban areas.

60. Which of the following is NOT true about a stanine score?

a. Stanine scores represent nine statistical units.
b. Stanine scores are based on a standard bell curve.
c. Stanine scores have a mean of five.
d. Stanine scores have a standard deviation of one.

61. A school counselor is working with the administrative team at her school to improve student behavior. Which of the following would be an appropriate type of analysis to use as a first step in creating a schoolwide behavior plan?

a. Mapping discipline incidents and disaggregating the data to look for trends
b. Making a list of students who frequently cause behavior problems to check in with daily
c. Sending a survey to teachers to identify their biggest behavioral concerns
d. Conducting a functional behavior assessment for students with discipline incidents

62. Mr. Dean, a school counseling student in a graduate program, is applying for internship positions for the upcoming school year and is required to carry professional liability insurance. What is the best method for Mr. Dean to acquire a complete professional liability policy?

a. Contact his university field experiences office
b. Contact the local school district to be added to their district policy
c. Join the National Board for Certified Counselors
d. Join ASCA as a student member

63. Which of the following examples demonstrates a school counselor acting as a consultant while working with a community agency?

a. A school counselor attends a session to learn about the services an agency provides that may benefit their students.
b. A school counselor attends a professional development session provided by an agency about working with students with anxiety.
c. A school counselor works with a therapist from an agency to develop a plan of care for a student in their school.
d. A school counselor discusses the strategies they are using with a student with the student's new therapist at an agency.

64. School counselors at all levels incorporate career standards into their programming. Which of the following career-related activities would be MOST appropriate at the elementary level?

a. A career day during which students can learn about different kinds of careers
b. Mapping steps through high school graduation toward college and career goals
c. Taking aptitude or personality quizzes geared toward career choices
d. Researching a career of interest and creating a poster about that career

Refer to the following for question 65:

Ms. White, a high school counselor, is planning a small group focused on improving study skills. As part of the group, she has students complete an electronic survey describing their independent use of various study skills in the first group meeting, and she plans to have them complete another survey in the last group meeting. After a few group sessions, she notices that one group member continually asks other students if they are doing their homework, using their study skills, and focusing in class.

This student reminds their peers that they are supposed to be doing their assignments and studying regularly.

65. Which type of data is Ms. White collecting with this survey?

a. Process data
b. Perception data
c. Outcome data
d. Quantitative data

66. Mrs. Mason is a high school counselor who has been working with a 9th-grade student in individual counseling for a month. During their first three sessions together, it becomes clear that the student has significant depression and has not experienced any improvement during the course of individual counseling thus far. Which of the following is the most appropriate next step for Mrs. Mason?

a. Sign up for a webinar about depression to learn new strategies to help the student.
b. Call a local mental health facility for a crisis evaluation on the student.
c. Seek professional advice from another school counselor in the district.
d. Work with the student and their parent to refer the child to an outside mental health provider.

67. A high school student experiences the death of their sibling a few days before they are scheduled to take the SAT. If the student takes the test as scheduled, which of the following is true?

a. Their test score will not be affected since the SAT is a validated assessment.
b. Their test score may not be reliable due to their emotional state.
c. Their test score may not be valid due to their emotional state.
d. Their test score will not be affected since the SAT does not measure social-emotional skills.

68. Which of the following documents provides an outline of objectives that can be used in planning a classroom guidance curriculum?

a. ASCA Ethical Standards for School Counselors
b. ASCA Mindsets & Behaviors for Student Success
c. ASCA National Model
d. Recognized ASCA Model Program

69. Which of the following is NOT a necessary condition for a successful collaborative relationship?

a. Active listening, trust, and clear communication
b. Establishing norms and expectations
c. Having a shared vision and goal
d. Having a defined group leader

70. Counselors leading group counseling sessions for students have an ethical obligation to obtain informed consent from all group participants. Which of the following is NOT a part of informed consent in a group counseling setting?

a. Limits of confidentiality
b. Parental consent
c. Knowing other group members
d. Purpose and goals of the group

71. Joshua is a 5th-grade student who is frequently disruptive and explosive in the classroom. School-wide and classroom-wide interventions, such as positive recognition, class-based rewards, and modifying classroom procedures to reduce opportunities for inappropriate behavior have not resulted in an improvement in Joshua's behavior. Joshua's school counselor is working with the administrative team to develop a behavior plan for him. What would be the best method for collecting data to support the development of this plan?

a. Asking Joshua's teacher to write a narrative about his behavior throughout the school year and the interventions put into place
b. Collecting all of the discipline incident reports generated when Joshua was suspended throughout the year and looking for patterns
c. Asking Joshua's parents to complete a behavior checklist, indicating the behaviors they are most concerned about
d. Conducting a functional behavior assessment to determine the purpose of Joshua's behavior and factors contributing to it

72. A school counselor is conducting a classroom guidance lesson, and two students, Brian and Kenny, are talking and giggling while the counselor is presenting. Which strategy should the counselor use first to manage their behavior?

a. Walk near the students and stand behind them while continuing the lesson.
b. Momentarily stop the lesson and say, "Brian and Kenny, please be quiet."
c. Momentarily stop the lesson and move Brian and Kenny's seats.
d. Ignore the students' behavior so as not to give them attention.

Refer to the following for question 73:

> A school counselor leading a counseling group for students whose parents are going through a separation or divorce generally sits and listens to the group's conversations but does not participate in the conversations or provide direction to the group.

73. Which group leadership style is this counselor demonstrating?

a. Autocratic
b. Democratic
c. Laissez-faire
d. Authoritarian

74. A school counselor is part of a school team tasked with developing an intervention plan for a 7th-grade student with severe social/emotional deficits and behavioral concerns. The team decides that, in order to understand the student's behavior, they must conduct an evaluation of the student's functioning in a variety of settings, including at school, at home with the immediate family, and in the community. The team's approach to evaluation best represents which of the following theories?

a. Bronfenbrenner's ecological systems theory
b. Bowen's family systems theory
c. Vygotsky's social development theory
d. Piaget's cognitive development theory

75. Which of the following is NOT an appropriate strategy for facilitating course selections for middle-school students?

a. Calling a grade-level meeting to discuss course options and having all students fill out a course selection form individually
b. Holding individual meetings with students and their parents to discuss their course options and make selections
c. Incorporating course selections into a classroom guidance lesson and having students fill out a course selection form during the lesson
d. Using grades and standardized test data to assign students to courses based on current achievement

76. Mrs. Jones is a high school counselor working with a student in individual counseling. The student is struggling with math class and recently received a failing grade on an exam. In the counseling session, the student makes the statement, "I failed my math test. I am so stupid!" If Mrs. Jones is taking a cognitive behavioral therapy-based approach with this student, which of the following would be an appropriate response to the student's statement?

a. Challenging the student's belief that they must be stupid if they received a failing grade on a test
b. Asking the student about their previous experiences with math tests to explore the root of the student's struggles
c. Asking the student if there has been a math test they performed well on and trying to identify what the student did differently on that test
d. Reflecting the student's statement, validating their feelings, and demonstrating unconditional positive regard for the student

77. A seven-year-old student is engaged in a classroom guidance session focused on friendship skills. The student comments that "It is important to take turns, otherwise you will get in trouble with the teacher." This student's comment best aligns with which stage of moral development, according to Lawrence Kohlberg?

a. Obedience and punishment (stage 1)
b. Maintaining personal relationships (stage 3)
c. Law and order (stage 4)
d. Social contract (stage 5)

78. Which of the following is NOT one of Holland's six basic personality types?

a. Investigative
b. Artistic
c. Social
d. Logical

79. Holland believed that a specific career will tend to attract people with similar personality types. One example would be the occupation of "teacher," which best aligns with which personality type?

a. Artistic
b. Conventional
c. Investigative
d. Social

80. Sophie is a 3rd-grade student who wrote in a class assignment that she wants to be a veterinarian when she grows up. Based on Ginzberg and associates' career development theory, which stage of career development is Sophie in?

a. Informal
b. Fantasy
c. Growth
d. Tentative

81. Ms. Silver is a school counselor whose program focuses on helping students develop the foundational skills and mindsets to become lifelong learners. She does a great deal of prevention and early intervention work and helps students develop strong social/emotional skills. Ms. Silver's programming best aligns with the counselor's role at which level?

a. Elementary school
b. Middle school
c. High school
d. K-12

82. Which of the following examples of a career assessment is an example of an interest assessment?

a. Myers-Briggs Type Indicator
b. Holland Code
c. ASVAB
d. Strong Interest Inventory

83. Ms. Martinez, a school counselor, receives a referral regarding a middle school student who was caught stealing food at school. Ms. Martinez meets with the student individually, and he tells her that he was hungry because he "doesn't get to eat at home" and "isn't allowed to eat when he is in trouble." Ms. Martinez also receives a report that, upon hearing of his disciplinary write-up, the student's sibling stated that he was lying about not being able to eat at home and that they both get plenty to eat. Which type of referral would be most appropriate for Ms. Martinez to make in this situation?

a. Ms. Martinez should refer the student to Child Protective Services due to suspicion of neglect, despite what the sibling stated.
b. Ms. Martinez should refer the student to child nutrition for an application for free lunch so that he doesn't get in trouble for taking food.
c. Ms. Martinez should refer the student to the principal, as this is a behavioral issue and not an issue of neglect.
d. Ms. Martinez should refer the student for additional individual counseling to address this behavior.

84. Which of the following is NOT an example of a criterion-referenced assessment?

a. End-of-grade exams
b. End-of-unit assessments
c. AP exams
d. The SAT

85. Which of the following is NOT true about trait-factor career counseling?

a. Trait-factor career counseling assumes that there is one best career for each individual.
b. Trait-factor career counseling is a developmental process for each individual.
c. Trait-factor career counseling relies on data from a variety of tests.
d. Trait-factor career counseling takes an individual's personality into account.

86. Which of the following types of programs is best supported by research for bullying prevention?

a. Disciplinary action and zero tolerance for bullying behaviors
b. Schoolwide programs focused on changing the behaviors of all students
c. Schoolwide or grade-level assemblies with motivational speakers
d. Assertiveness training for victims of bullying

87. The requirement for school counseling program evaluations and school counseling program accountability is discussed in all of the following documents EXCEPT:

a. The ASCA National Model
b. ASCA Ethical Standards for School Counselors
c. ASCA Mindsets & Behaviors for Student Success
d. ASCA School Counselor Professional Standards & Competencies

88. A high school counselor spends 20 minutes on the phone with a student's mental health therapist, discussing how school personnel can help to ensure the safety of the student after a recent mental health crisis. This is an example of which type of task?

a. Individual student planning
b. Responsive services
c. Consultation
d. Creating an action plan

89. Ms. McCoy is leading a counseling group for children whose parents are going through a divorce or separation. Which of the following would NOT be a goal of this type of support group?

a. Allowing children to share their feelings about their family situation
b. Allowing children to discuss the changes that are happening in their family
c. Allowing children to be reassured and feel hopeful about their situation
d. Allowing children to practice conflict resolution strategies and communication skills

90. A student was referred to the counselor after having an outburst of anger during class. When asked about the situation that led to the outburst, the student says, "My teacher made me mad because they gave me lunch detention for arriving to class late. But it's not fair because another teacher was talking to me in the hallway and made me late!" Which part of the student's statement indicates the "B" part of the ABC model, according to cognitive behavioral therapy?

a. The student arrived to class late.
b. The teacher issued a consequence of lunch detention to the student.
c. The student thought the consequence was unfair.
d. The student felt angry.

91. Counseling program evaluations serve a variety of purposes for both the school counseling program and the profession as a whole. Which of the following is NOT a purpose served by school counseling program evaluations?

a. Sharing results with stakeholders
b. Advocating for the needs of the counseling program
c. Identifying future program goals
d. Advocating for a pay raise

92. Jake, a middle school student, makes a comment in class that he wishes he was "never born." The teacher refers Jake to the counselor based on his comment. What is the appropriate response for the school counselor in this scenario?

a. Call the crisis response number for a mental health evaluation.
b. Talk with Jake about making inappropriate comments in class.
c. Talk with Jake about his comments, and call his parents to let them know what he said.
d. Conduct a suicide screening, and determine the severity of Jake's threat.

Refer to the following for question 93:

Mrs. Johnson is a middle school counselor who has been working with a seventh-grade student in individual counseling. The student was diagnosed by an outside therapist with an anxiety disorder and regularly earns failing grades on tests despite excellent classwork and homework grades. Mrs. Johnson convenes a team meeting to discuss appropriate accommodations for the student under Section 504. Since she has other students that also struggle with anxiety disorders, she is also considering adding the student to a small counseling group.

93. Which of the following would NOT be a benefit to utilizing small group counseling for this purpose?

a. Meeting with more students at one time
b. Opportunities for peer modeling
c. Lower anxiety levels in a group setting
d. Opportunities for social exposure

94. Which of the following is NOT an example of consultation?

a. A school counselor meets with a student's parents to share strategies to support their child's success.
b. A school counselor discusses a student's recent testing with the school psychologist to learn about their results.
c. A school counselor and teacher meet to come up with strategies that they can both use to support a specific student.
d. A school counselor meets with a community agency to learn about the services they can provide to students.

95. In designing a comprehensive school counseling program, which of the following types of student development would NOT be a major focus of the guidance program?

a. Learning strategies
b. Self-management skills
c. Social skills
d. Emotional regulation skills

96. Which of the following describes a method a school counselor could utilize to collect perception data in order to measure the effectiveness of a closing-the-gap action plan?

a. Comparing schoolwide academic data from before and after the intervention
b. Comparing pre- and post-tests of the student competencies targeted during the intervention
c. Completing sign-in sheets to track attendance at each portion of the intervention
d. Collecting schoolwide student surveys from before and after the intervention

97. Which of the following is true regarding standardized test scores of students who are learning English as a second language?

a. If tests are translated into the students' native language, student scores are valid.
b. Student scores are likely to be invalid due to language and cultural differences.
c. Standardized test scores are a reliable measure of English proficiency.
d. Standardized test scores are invalid if the test is translated into another language.

98. Which of the following does NOT describe an appropriate role for a school counselor in addressing eating disorders?

a. Implementing cognitive behavioral therapy in individual counseling
b. Recognizing the signs and symptoms of a potential eating disorder
c. Implementing preventative curriculum for parents and students
d. Facilitating referrals to outside agencies or programs for treatment

99. Which of the following physical and growth changes best align with the physical developmental stage known as early adulthood?

a. Rapid physical growth
b. Development of primary sex characteristics
c. Development of secondary sex characteristics
d. Peak physical strength

100. Mr. Smith, a school counselor, is serving on an IEP team for a student with severe social-emotional needs. The IEP team brings up the need for the student to have individual counseling focused on these needs. Which of the following statements would be an appropriate response from Mr. Smith in this situation?

a. It is inappropriate for a school counselor to provide individual counseling to a student as part of their IEP, as they are not certified special education staff.
b. It is appropriate for a school counselor to provide individual counseling to a student as part of their IEP, but no more than once per week.
c. It is inappropriate for a school counselor to provide individual counseling to a student as part of their IEP, as it is not an approved special education service.
d. It is appropriate for a school counselor to provide individual counseling to a student as part of their IEP, but only on a short-term basis for a specific goal.

101. Which of the following is true about solution-focused brief therapy?

a. In solution-focused brief therapy, the counselor must understand the client's problem before beginning to work on solving it.
b. Solution-focused brief therapy is appropriate when the client is unable to articulate their desired goal.
c. Solution-focused brief therapy requires the client to make major changes in their daily lives.
d. Solution-focused brief therapy does not require the client to have a mental health diagnosis to begin counseling.

102. Adam, a 6th-grade student, was referred to his school counselor by his mother, who noted in her referral that Adam was acting more emotional than usual at home. The school counselor meets with Adam several times in individual counseling, where they discuss coping strategies and stress management skills. A few weeks later, Adam's mother emails the counselor asking what they discussed in counseling. Which response is the most appropriate according to the ASCA Ethical Standards for School Counselors?

a. The counselor replies to the email, saying that she received the referral but cannot comment on any follow-up made.
b. The counselor calls the mother and shares what she has discussed with Adam since the parent has a right to information about her child.
c. The counselor emails the mother back to share what she discussed in counseling since the parent has a right to information about her child.
d. The counselor calls the mother on the phone and shares that she has met with Adam on several occasions but cannot provide details without Adam's permission.

103. Mr. Hunter, a high school counselor, assembles an advisory council consisting of teachers, parents, students, his building principals, and local community members. He meets with members of this advisory council two times per year to review goals and student outcomes for the counseling program. With which component of the ASCA National Model program does this activity most closely align?

a. Define
b. Manage
c. Deliver
d. Assess

104. A 2nd-grade student recently mastered the skill of adding two-digit numbers. His teacher knows that, because of his mastery of addition, he is ready to learn the process of subtracting two-digit numbers with her support and guidance. The teacher is basing her understanding of the student's learning on which concept?

a. Assimilation and accommodation
b. Zone of proximal development
c. Social learning
d. Classical conditioning

105. Which of the following scenarios is in violation of the Family Educational Rights and Privacy Act (FERPA)?

a. A 16-year-old student asks to view their educational record and is permitted to do so without parental consent.
b. A non-custodial parent asks to inspect their child's educational record and is permitted to do so without the custodial parent's consent.
c. A parent asks to review their child's educational record and then requests an item that they believe to be inaccurate be removed from the record.
d. A school creates a directory of student contact information and allows parents a 30-day notice to opt out of the directory.

106. Frank Parsons, "The Father of Guidance," is best known for his contributions to the school counseling profession focusing on which counseling role?

a. Therapeutic counseling
b. Vocational counseling
c. Promoting systemic change
d. Advocating for the profession

107. Leslie is a middle school counselor who has an upcoming planning meeting with the counselor at the elementary school where the majority of Leslie's students attended. The purpose of the meeting is to begin planning for a successful middle school transition for Leslie's future students. Which of the following topics would likely NOT be discussed in this meeting?

a. Strategies for helping students take responsibility for their learning (study skills and organization)
b. Strategies for helping students integrate into their new school (clubs and activities)
c. An overview of the course selection, the registration process, and the data needed to complete selections
d. The IEP goals and services for EC students who will be entering Leslie's school next year

108. When administering a standardized test, such as an end-of-grade test, certain conditions must be maintained in order for the test results to be valid. Which of the following conditions would NOT impact the validity of a standardized end-of-grade reading test?

a. Altering the length of time provided for the test
b. Changing the number of items on the test
c. Explaining a test question in simpler terms
d. Administering the test at a different time of day

109. Mr. Lowe, a classroom teacher, meets with the school counselor to discuss a student, Erin. Erin has a diagnosis of generalized anxiety disorder (GAD), and Mr. Lowe is seeking information about how to help mitigate the impact of anxiety on Erin's classroom behavior. During their meeting, the counselor shares general information about GAD as well as common strategies and techniques that classroom teachers use to support students with this diagnosis. Their meeting could best be described as which of the following?

a. Consultation
b. Collaboration
c. Professional development
d. Referral

110. A school counselor is evaluating end-of-grade assessments for 3rd grade reading at their school. The mean of the scores is 50. What does a mean of 50 represent?

a. The average test score is 50.
b. The highest test score is 50.
c. The most common test score is 50.
d. The percentage of students who passed the test is 50.

111. Alex is a middle school student who struggles with focus and attention in class. Alex's difficulties frequently result in incomplete work and poor grades on assessments. Alex's 504 team determined that he would benefit from preferential seating and extended time on assignments. Which of the following terms best describes preferential seating and extended time?

a. Intervention
b. Accommodation
c. Modification
d. Instruction

112. A counselor is researching best practices for working with a family whose children witnessed a violent crime and are now experiencing anxiety, having difficulty focusing, showing physical illness, and displaying inappropriate behavior. Which of the following research-based approaches would this counselor most likely consider in working with these children?

a. Family system therapy
b. Trauma-informed practices
c. Multi-tiered systems of support
d. Positive behavior intervention and support

113. Which of the following is NOT true about the use of advisory councils in an ASCA National Model program?

a. Advisory councils must meet quarterly each school year.
b. Advisory councils can assist the school counselor in reviewing program results.
c. Advisory councils should include students and parents.
d. Advisory councils should be smaller than 20 members.

114. Which of the following questions is answered by the school counseling program evaluation?

a. "How are students different as a result of the school counseling program?"
b. "What measurable progress have students made toward counseling program objectives?"
c. "How effective is the school counseling program in achieving its stated goals?"
d. "What impact has the school counseling program had on academic achievement?"

115. Mrs. Navarro is a school counselor who has put together a plan of strategies to support a specific student at a classroom teacher's request. Mrs. Navarro observes the student in the classroom, collects data about their academic performance, and then meets with their teacher to present a plan to support the student in the classroom. Which mode of consultation has Mrs. Navarro engaged in this situation?

a. Prescriptive mode
b. Mediation mode
c. Provision mode
d. Initiation mode

116. Mrs. Harris, a school counselor, is approached by a teacher at her school who asks her if she has a moment to talk. The teacher then shares with Mrs. Harris that she is having conflict in her family and is struggling mentally and emotionally with her situation. She asks Mrs. Harris if she can provide individual counseling to help her through this difficult time. What would be an appropriate next step for Mrs. Harris?

a. Mrs. Harris should listen empathetically but ultimately provide the teacher with a list of referral resources to find a counselor outside of school.
b. Mrs. Harris should listen and set up regular times to meet with the teacher to talk because the teacher's mental health impacts students.
c. Mrs. Harris should steer the conversation away from the teacher's personal problems and should only discuss academic concerns with her.
d. Mrs. Harris should discuss the teacher's situation with HR because they can provide information about the school's mental health insurance benefits.

117. A 7th-grade student takes a standardized achievement test in math and receives a score of "not proficient." All of the following are possible interpretations of the student's score, EXCEPT:

a. The student did not demonstrate mastery of established grade-level standards for math.
b. The student did not receive appropriate instruction in all of the grade-level standards for math.
c. The student demonstrated a lower level of intelligence than their same-grade peers.
d. The student demonstrated mastery of some grade-level standards for math, but not all.

118. As part of a comprehensive school counseling program, a counselor outlines the focus of the program for the upcoming school year and formally discusses the alignment of the counseling program goals and school goals with their administrator. Which tool from the Management component accomplishes these goals?

a. Annual agreement
b. Advisory council
c. Annual calendar
d. Curriculum plan

119. According to ASCA, which of the following is true about the school counselor's role in educating students with disabilities?

a. The school counselor is best equipped to coordinate the writing and implementation of plans under Section 504.
b. The school counselor can be utilized for long-term individual counseling, but only with plans that are written under Section 504 and IDEA.
c. The school counselor's role is primarily focused on advocating for the legal rights of students with disabilities.
d. The school counselor is the best primary contact for identifying students with suspected disabilities.

120. Mr. Powell is a high school counselor in a rural area where families live up to an hour away from the school and many of his students are aspiring first-generation college students. He plans to host a FAFSA workshop prior to the upcoming submission deadline. Which strategy should Mr. Powell consider to encourage the MOST parent participation in his workshop?

a. Hold the FAFSA workshop during the school day for students to attend and provide copies of the slide show presentation for students to give to their parents
b. Post a link to the FAFSA application on the school website with a reminder about the upcoming deadline
c. Hold a FAFSA workshop in the evening and video record the instructional portion of the event for parents who can't attend in person
d. Utilize the school's student information system to send an email to parents reminding them of the deadline and directing them to the school website for the link

Answer Key and Explanations for Test #1

1. A: A statistical trend is a method of measuring a change over time. There are a variety of methods and tests that can be utilized to analyze statistical trends. If a statistically significant trend exists within a set of data (such as graduation rates over the course of multiple years), then that trend could be understood as the overall direction of data. In the example described, there could be a trend toward increasing or decreasing graduation rates. It is also possible to have no trend within a data set. The mean is the average of the data, which is not helpful in analyzing changes over time in this example. The mode is the most common value within the data, and the standard deviation has to do with distribution along a bell curve, neither of which are helpful pieces of information for the example given.

2. C: School counselors have an ethical obligation to report suspected abuse in accordance with state and local policies. It is not the role of the counselor to investigate potential child abuse or determine if abuse is happening before making a report. If a mandated reporter just suspects abuse, neglect or exploitation, they are obligated to file a report.

3. C: When it comes to student behavior, there is typically a great deal of both perception and outcome data. Perception data is the type of data described in answer choices A, B, and D, and focuses on what students or staff know or believe about student behavior. Perception data is subjective and cannot be the only type of data used to evaluate an intervention. Outcome data, such as the number of disciplinary referrals, number of days of suspensions issued, or number of disciplinary incidents broken down by type, can be analyzed to evaluate the effectiveness of an intervention aimed at improving student behavior or decreasing disciplinary incidents.

4. B: Scheduling some type of downtime during the day is an effective way to manage job stress. Saving work for time at home will only create more stress in the long run. Asking to eliminate fair-share duties is not appropriate to ask of her principal, as fair-share duties are necessary for the school to function and are shared equally among staff members. Canceling classroom guidance sessions will result in students missing critical curriculum components.

5. B: In this scenario, small group counseling would be an appropriate strategy based on the data, specific issues, and number of students. Individual counseling sessions may wind up being appropriate for some of the students in the lower-attendance group, but a small group intervention would make more efficient use of the counselor's time and is more appropriate as an intermediate intervention. Proactive classroom guidance lessons are appropriate in addressing attendance, but based on the data presented, the counselor is past the point of implementing a proactive intervention. Most teachers likely already understand the importance of school attendance, and acting as a consultant to provide information on this topic likely wouldn't have a direct impact on student attendance. However, collaboration with the teacher to develop strategies and incentives that may improve attendance in this classroom may be appropriate.

6. D: Only academic, career, and social/emotional domains are included in the ASCA Mindsets & Behaviors for Student Success. College readiness is a part of the Career domain; however, it is not the primary focus.

7. A: Primary prevention groups are meant to prevent mental health concerns from arising. A social skills group would fall into this category. Secondary prevention groups are meant to address mental health concerns that have developed but are not yet serious or life-threatening, such as anger or stress management. Finally, tertiary prevention groups address serious or life-threatening mental health concerns, such as eating disorders and alcoholism.

8. C: School counselors, while trained in individual counseling techniques and mental health issues, are not mental health counselors. It is inappropriate for counselors to provide long-term individual counseling or mental health counseling in schools. In addition, school counselors cannot make mental health diagnoses or treat a mental health condition. In the scenario described, Mr. Hyde has already provided a great deal of individual counseling to this student; a general rule of thumb is that if a student requires more than six sessions of individual counseling for a single issue, a referral is likely warranted. A small group may be beneficial for Anna, but the length of time and severity of her concern warrants professional help. Mr. Hyde should follow his school and/or district policy in providing Anna's parents/guardians with a referral for mental health counseling.

9. C: Based on this one data point, targeted intervention for 7th-grade students is the most appropriate option. If an entire grade level is lagging behind others in terms of attendance rates, a small group intervention does not target the group of students whose outcome data is lagging. Choices A and D could be important additional perception data points in designing an intervention, but they are not interventions in themselves.

10. A: Norm-referenced tests compare an individual's test score to those of a comparison group, typically a group of same-age or same-grade peers. For many state-standardized tests, a child's individual score is compared to a norm group of students across the state, and sometimes there are additional norm groups for the school or district. Parents who are trying to understand their child's test scores may confuse a percentile rank with a percentage of correct answers on the test itself, but they are very different data points. Norm-referenced tests compare an individual's performance to a comparison group, while criterion-referenced tests compare an individual's performance to a set of standards or objectives to be mastered. End-of-grade tests often do measure a student's mastery of grade-level standards, but the indication that this child's test score is from a "norm-referenced" test means that their results are calculated in comparison with their peers.

11. B: In this situation, the counselor's goal should be to stop the inappropriate conversation. Gossiping about others who are not in the group is not helpful to the group or appropriate in the context of the group. Blocking is a strategy for stopping a hurtful behavior. Clarification, linking, and active listening would all be inappropriate choices in this scenario because they would invite the student to continue their line of discussion.

12. D: Students who identify as LGBTQ are more likely to have poor grades and patterns of truancy than their heterosexual peers. Students in this group also report feeling less safe at school and are more likely to be bullied, all factors that can aggravate academic outcomes. Studies have found that some of these impacts are significant. These are important trends for school counselors to be aware of. Effective school counselors can help LGBTQ youth to establish protective factors (such as connecting with peers or school staff) that can mitigate some of these potential negative impacts and help create a safe learning environment for all students through advocacy.

13. D: Program outcome data provides information on the direct impacts of the school counseling program on student outcomes. When combined with program process and perception data, outcome data helps a school counselor create a clear picture of their program over the course of a school year. The school data profile and closing-the-gap action plan results can help clarify goals for the next school year, but the outcome data provides information that is most directly related to the school counseling program to identify areas for improvement.

14. C: The use-of-time assessment is a document that helps school counselors determine how much of their time is spent in each of the components of the ASCA National Model, including the breakdown of direct and indirect services. The ideal breakdown of time is 80% spent on direct and indirect student services, while the remaining 20% goes to school support and program management. While many school counselors could estimate their use of time and enter that information into a survey or Excel spreadsheet, a calendar such as Google Calendar would be more likely to help counselors accurately calculate their use of time. The school's student information system may have helpful information about student use of time or fair-share duties, depending on how the school uses the program, but this would not be as useful as the digital calendar. Sick time documentation would not help counselors determine how they are using the time they are at school.

15. D: Counselors frequently make referrals to connect their students with appropriate resources to support their needs. Counselors may make internal referrals, which include referrals to school staff such as the nurse, principal, psychologist, intervention team, and so forth. Answer choices A, B, and C all give examples of internal referrals. Choices A and B are examples of appropriate referrals, while choice C is not appropriate for the student's needs. Students expressing suicidal ideation should be evaluated by a mental health professional and referred in accordance with school and district policies; school psychologists are typically not qualified mental health providers. External referrals could be made to community resources, social services, mental health organizations, or any other person or service that takes place outside of the school environment.

16. A: Assertiveness training groups are typically highly structured and focus on practicing skills learned in the group through role-playing. Linking and encouraging may be used in many types of groups, so it is not specific to an assertiveness training cognitive behavioral therapy (CBT) group. The empty chair technique could be used in assertiveness training, but it is a Gestalt technique, not a CBT technique.

17. B: Outcome data is the data that measures the positive impact of the intervention. In the case of a small group focused on improving attendance, students' attendance rates at the conclusion of the small group represent a measurable impact. Meeting logs tracking student attendance at the small group meetings would be an example of process data, while post-tests and self-evaluations would both be examples of perception data.

18. A: The ASVAB is an aptitude test designed to measure a student's strengths in relation to potential careers in the military. As the name suggests, aptitude tests are designed to measure an individual's aptitude or potential for success. Aptitude tests are frequently used in career planning or guidance, as many examples of aptitude tests (such as the ASVAB, Holland Code Career Aptitude Test, and Myers-Briggs Career Type Indicator) point test-takers to certain careers or fields based on their individual strengths. End-of-grade tests are an example of an achievement test, or one which measures what the test-taker has learned. The SAT, while originally designed as an aptitude test, was redesigned in 2016 and is now another example of an achievement test. The TOEFL is a proficiency test that measures the test-taker's English language ability as compared to a general standard.

19. C: The activities described would best apply to the working or norming stage of a small group. For this activity, students have already been selected and screened, established group norms, and begun the work of the group. They are working toward the goals established and learning the skills to help them there.

20. B: It is common for school counselors to encounter situations where students require referrals to mental health agencies for counseling to occur outside of school. School counselors have training and skills in individual counseling and mental health, but it is inappropriate for counselors to provide long-term individual counseling, diagnose mental health disorders, or treat mental health disorders in school. In situations where students require those services, referrals can be necessary. According to ASCA, it is most appropriate for school counselors to provide families with a pre-approved or pre-screened list of agency referrals provided by the school or district. This helps protect the counselor from liability and also protects the privacy of students and families; providing names of agencies utilized by other students in the same school could create privacy concerns for those students. In situations when students are in crisis, emergency mental health screenings may be appropriate depending on school and district policy, but they are not appropriate to utilize in all situations.

21. C: According to the ASCA National Model, it is inappropriate for school counselors to be responsible for school-wide coordination of individual student intervention plans or other individual student plans, such as attendance plans, student review teams, or IEPs. Each of the other tasks or duties is appropriate and utilizes the strengths and training of the school counselor to contribute to an effective MTSS committee.

22. C: The use-of-time assessment tool can be utilized in this scenario to demonstrate the appropriate tasks completed by Mrs. Lewis and the amount of time dedicated to each of those tasks, which in turn could help her advocate for continuing the appropriate use of her time. The annual agreement can guide Mrs. Lewis and her building principal to determine appropriate tasks and role expectations at the onset of the school year. The other answer choices include ASCA National Model tools, but those tools do not focus on appropriate tasks and use of time and would be less likely to be effectively utilized in this scenario.

23. A: The situation described is social bullying. Melissa is being excluded, and her relationships with friends and classmates are being damaged by rumors and exclusion. Social bullying is also called relational aggression. Verbal bullying includes name-calling, threats, mean comments, or jokes at the expense of another person. Physical bullying includes hitting, kicking, fighting, tripping, or other types of physical harm. Cyberbullying is bullying behavior that takes place online or through screens and can incorporate other types of bullying, such as social and verbal bullying.

24. A: Process data describes the school counseling program in terms of who was served and how. In other words, process data tells when and how often programming occurred and how many students participated. This type of data would be supportive for a counselor advocating for an appropriate student-to-counselor ratio, especially if their process data demonstrates that they are unable to reach all of the students on their caseload equally or their caseload is much larger than the recommended 250:1. Outcome and perception data is more likely to be utilized to support a request for professional development for counselors or teachers. Other types of data, such as the use-of-time assessment or published research on the training and impact of school counselors, could be used to advocate for reassignment of inappropriate duties.

25. B: Solution-focused brief counseling always focuses on the exception to the problem, improvements since the previous session, and progress toward the goal. Therefore, most subsequent sessions will begin with the counselor asking the client about what has improved since the previous session.

26. A: Even though termination is the final stage of the group counseling process, an effective group leader will begin to prepare group members for the termination in the selection and screening process by explaining the duration and goals of the group.

27. B: When determining group size, it is important to keep in mind the goals of the group as well as the age of the participants. Participants should have the opportunity to share and participate regularly, lest they lose interest or feel frustrated at waiting for their turn; they should also have ample opportunity to practice new skills to cement their new knowledge. Adult groups could successfully maintain a larger number of participants (up to 12, but 10 or fewer is ideal), but younger children require a smaller group. Four to six is a typical group size for elementary-age children.

28. A: Contracts or pledges to refrain from drug/alcohol use are generally not very effective, just like with suicide contracts. ASCA and the National Institute on Drug Abuse discuss the evidence-based best practices for drug abuse prevention. Factual education about the risks and effects of drug/alcohol use, especially the effects of drug/alcohol use on the adolescent brain, is an effective component of a comprehensive program. A stress management component is important because many students view drug/alcohol use as a means to reduce or cope with stress. Many evidence-based programs include components and education designed to reduce risk factors (such as aggressive behavior and poverty) and boost protective factors (such as self-control and academic competence). While schools do not always have control over the risk factors students may have, a comprehensive program can strengthen the protective factors, which can mitigate the effects of those risk factors.

29. B: Classroom guidance is the only component that fits the criteria described in the question. All students benefit from the developmentally appropriate curriculum provided by the school counselor during classroom guidance lessons. In fact, this systematic method of reaching all students is one of the main benefits of providing a classroom guidance curriculum. For ASCA Mindsets and Behaviors, which all students are expected to demonstrate mastery of, classroom guidance provides a method to reach each student.

30. B: Analyzing a results report is part of the Assess component of the ASCA National Model, not the Manage component. Results reports are used to evaluate the effectiveness of classroom instruction, small-group services to students, and closing-the-gap action plans. Completing a use-of-time assessment, creating a closing-the-gap action plan, and writing a mission and vision statement are all part of the effective management of a comprehensive school counseling program. These activities help counselors clarify the needs of their school and students and define priorities for their program.

31. C: In most schools, the school psychologist is an appropriate member of a team when a child has progressed through the initial stages of intervention and is being considered for a special education evaluation. In the scenario described with Adam, the team is conducting an initial intervention meeting, so psychological or educational testing would likely not yet be appropriate, and the school psychologist would not yet be involved.

32. A: Understanding the limits of confidentiality is a necessary part of informed consent, which should be established in the selection/screening process. Even though the expectations regarding confidentiality are addressed in the initial/forming stage of the group counseling process, the initial disclosure of the limits of those expectations should take place prior to the initial group session.

33. A: Particularly with a group focused on social skills with students who struggle with appropriate social behavior, the individual interview is an extremely important part of the group selection process. Since all of the identified students are already known to struggle with social skills, it is necessary to interview each student to determine their current level of functioning with the skills necessary for group participation, such as active listening and turn-taking. Answer D, conducting an individual counseling session to practice group skills, may be appropriate for some group members after determining the final makeup of the group.

34. C: Linking is a strategy specifically for identifying "links" or commonalities between group members. Linking can help group members feel connected to one another and improve overall cohesion and interaction in the group.

35. A: A tiered intervention model layers interventions from tier I (broad, whole-school or whole-class interventions), to tier II (more intensive, small-group interventions) and tier III (highly individualized, intensive interventions). Tier I can also be thought of as high-quality instructional practices provided to all students, while tiers II and III are layered on top of tier I. Because the classroom guidance curriculum is high-quality instruction provided to all students, it would be considered a tier I intervention. Small group counseling could be considered tier II, and individual counseling could be considered tier III, in terms of the levels of individual attention and intensity of interventions described by the tiered intervention model. A closing-the-gap action plan could certainly be part of a school's intervention planning, but it is not an intervention in and of itself; the action plan would describe interventions to be implemented for at-risk groups of students.

36. B: An individual counseling results report is not an actual report used by school counselors. Each of the other major components of a school counseling program is evaluated with a results report that corresponds with the action plan created for that component. A curriculum action plan is evaluated with a curriculum results report, a small group action plan is evaluated with a small group results report, and a closing-the-gap action plan is evaluated with a closing-the-gap results report. Each of these results reports includes process, perception, and outcome data in order to evaluate program components.

37. B: The needs assessment is part of evaluating school and student strengths and areas for improvement, which is included in the Management component of the ASCA National Model. Using technology in the form of a survey is a common and effective way to conduct a needs assessment because it allows for easy data analysis and dissemination. When conducting a needs assessment using an online or electronic survey, counselors should keep in mind issues of confidentiality in how the survey platform is used. In addition, counselors may want to consider their liability to respond to information shared in the assessment (such as revelations of abuse or suicidal ideation).

38. A: "Unaccompanied youth" is a demographic of students that frequently qualify for protections and services under the McKinney-Vento Homeless Assistance Act. According to McKinney-Vento's guidance, unaccompanied youth can qualify for these protections and services even if they ran away from their parents' home. The school's McKinney-Vento liaison is responsible for determining the student's eligibility for these protections and services and implementing them. Like all other information, a student's status as "homeless" or "unaccompanied youth" is confidential information and should only be shared with other school staff on an as-needed basis. It may be that Marcus needs assistance with time and materials for homework completion, but the level of information shared with teachers to get that type of support should be carefully considered to protect Marcus's confidentiality. For many students who are "unaccompanied youth," returning home may not be a safe option, so calling the police or Marcus's parents should be carefully considered in an ethical decision-making process.

39. B: An educational group is one that is designed to teach information and develop skills, regardless of the topic. Therefore, a group that teaches parenting skills would be considered an educational group. A group that focuses on processing a common experience of grief and loss would be an example of a support group, while the group planning a school event would be a task group. Finally, the group focused on overcoming test anxiety would be considered a counseling or therapy group.

40. C: One major benefit of ASCA membership is access to their extensive research database, including research on counselor effectiveness, best practices, and student outcomes. Each of the other resources mentioned may have this type of research, but ASCA will have the most extensive collection for counselors.

41. B: All of the topics mentioned are important topics for a high school counselor to discuss with seniors, but not all are appropriate for a grade-level meeting format. Grade-level meetings are best for topics where information is standardized for all students and basic information needs to be shared quickly. Answer choice A, study skills and improving grades, would be better in group counseling or classroom guidance so that the counselor could address individual needs and goals. Answer choice C, dating violence prevention, would be better in classroom guidance where the counselor can better monitor student reactions and address comments and questions in a more confidential setting. Answer choice D, NCAA eligibility requirements, would not apply to every student in a single grade level, so it would not be a good use of the students' time to have a grade-level meeting on that topic.

42. C: Validity refers to a test's ability to measure what it was intended to measure. For example, a state end-of-grade reading assessment is valid if it measures reading standards for that grade level. Reliability, on the other hand, refers to how consistent a test is. That same end-of-grade reading assessment would be reliable if the same student achieved the same results on the test on different days. If a test is valid, it is usually also reliable; however, a test can be reliable without being valid. If an average 3rd grader who takes a college-level reading assessment consistently performs poorly on the assessment, the low score is reliable, but if the test was meant to measure mastery of 3rd-grade reading standards, it would not be valid. Validity does not depend on the number of questions answered correctly or the approval of a test under various laws or testing requirements.

43. A: Restlessness, difficulty concentrating, irritability, difficulty sleeping, headaches, stomachaches, and constant worry persisting for more than six months are all symptoms of generalized anxiety disorder. No core symptoms of ASD are present, and the physical symptoms like headaches and stomachaches are not consistent with ODD or ADHD.

44. D: According to ASCA, school counselors work with and advocate for the needs of students with special needs in a variety of ways, including being part of the IEP team. It is not appropriate for a counselor to lead the IEP team, coordinate special education, administer educational testing or assessments, or make sole determinations regarding IEP qualifications; however, it is appropriate for a school counselor to collaborate with the IEP team to advocate for the child's needs, ensure that the plan is appropriate, and help parents and students understand the plan.

45. B: Although FERPA permits sharing academic information within the school for staff with a "legitimate educational interest," outside agencies do not qualify for this permission. Although sharing this information with the case manager would probably directly benefit the student by assisting the tutoring program with identifying areas of need, the counselor must have parental consent to share this information with any outside agency. Having the student choose whether to provide this information is not appropriate, especially if they are a minor.

46. C: Process data focuses on the implementation of an intervention, such as the number of students who participated or the evidence of the intervention itself. Perception data describes what the participants of an intervention believe or think they have gained as a result of the intervention. Outcome data describes the measurable impact of an intervention, such as a gain in skills or abilities or improvements toward a specific goal. Answer choice C describes process data, not outcome data.

47. D: It is important for Ms. Meadows to help mitigate any potential problems with online communication by educating her students on the appropriate use of communication technology and boundaries, as well as understanding the nuances of online communication that could impact the counseling relationship (such as the inability to hear the tone of voice). The ASCA Ethical Standards for School Counselors specifically address virtual/online schooling, but there are no separate ASCA Ethical Standards for online/virtual school counselors. Ultimately, virtual/online school counselors are responsible for upholding the same ethical standards as those employed in traditional schools. The ASCA Ethical Standards state that counselors should inform parents and students of the limitations and differences in the online counseling relationship, including best practices for maintaining confidentiality. Additionally, the ASCA Ethical Standards indicate that virtual counselors should establish and communicate a method for accessing emergency assistance if the counselor is not available.

48. D: Commonly used intelligence tests are frequently criticized for having cultural biases that impact an individual's outcome; in addition, intelligence tests are known to measure a very limited type of intelligence. Even with these limitations, intelligence tests can be a helpful tool when utilized as a part of a broader assessment of an individual. For example, when evaluating students for special education services, a child's score on the Wechsler Intelligence Scale for Children may indicate relative strengths and weaknesses in different measurements of intelligence, which can help pinpoint specific learning disabilities. It is important to keep in mind, however, the criticism of these tests for being culturally biased and understand that they may not measure intelligence in the same way across different cultures. Like most assessments, intelligence tests should not be used as the only data point for decision making.

49. D: The ASCA National Model recommends that a counselor spend 80% or more of their time in the Delivery component of the program. This time can consist of both direct and indirect services. The remaining 20% is comprised of the Define, Manage, and Assess components.

50. B: The type of behavior described in this scenario would most likely occur in the transition/storming stage of group counseling. This stage is characterized by conflict and confrontation as the group members develop trust in the group process.

51. A: The annual calendar identifies the major activities of the school counseling program and publishes them in a manner that is accessible to stakeholders. The annual calendar can be used by the school counselor to increase the visibility of their comprehensive school counseling program and help stakeholders understand the components of the program. Activities include classroom guidance lessons, parent nights, student or class meeting dates, standardized test dates, college information meetings or application deadlines, and family activities.

The annual agreement is an ASCA National Model document that is used to outline the school counseling program and establish a formal agreement between the school counselor and school administration regarding counseling program goals. It is typically not a document that stakeholders outside of the counselor and principal have access to. The school data profile is a template used by the school counselor to identify areas of strength and need in their student achievement and behavior data, which can then be used to create action plans or program goals. Finally, a curriculum action plan is a document used by the school counselor to design the classroom guidance program and align the program with curricular goals, but this is not a document that is typically communicated to various stakeholders.

52. C: The student information system (SIS) is a very important resource for data-driven school counselors. Many data points essential to program evaluation activities can be found within this system, including individual, subgroup, and schoolwide data. Outcome data, in particular, is usually found within the SIS, including attendance rates, promotion and retention rates, graduation rates, student grade point averages, discipline referrals, suspensions, test scores, and so on. Process data, such as the information described in answer choice C, and perception data are typically harder to pull from the SIS and are more likely to be found in surveys, pre- and post-tests, sign-in sheets, needs assessments, and so forth. Each of these types of data is essential to a comprehensive program evaluation.

53. B: Standardized tests are a common experience and data point for schools across the country, and many schools and districts have used the results of these tests in all of the ways described in the answer choices. However, ASCA warns against placing too strong of an emphasis on individual test scores. Standardized tests provide only one data point in making decisions about curriculum, instruction, and the education of individual students. School counselors advocate for the use of multiple measures of student progress in making decisions about advanced or remedial coursework, intervention services, promotion, and retention. School counselors also advocate for the use of multiple measures in guiding school improvement, curriculum development, or instructional coaching. Standardized test scores can provide valuable information about academic achievement or school improvement, especially when the data is disaggregated by subgroup or compared to a norm-referenced group. However, this data should not be the sole or even primary data point in making decisions about students.

54. C: Personality assessments, such as the Myers-Briggs Type Indicator, can be useful tools for a variety of purposes, including self-reflection, learning coping skills, and identifying areas of academic or career interest. They are not, however, diagnostic assessments to be used for diagnosing personality disorders, evaluating for learning disabilities, or determining placement in special education or honors coursework. Personality assessments like the MBTI require an individual to be able to accurately reflect on and interpret their own thoughts, feelings, and behaviors and rate them accurately, and therefore should never be utilized as a sole data point in decision-making.

55. B: Mentor-mentee programs are a well-researched intervention for students at-risk. Tier I interventions are school-wide programs designed to provide quality instruction and support for all students. "At-risk" students, such as those who are failing courses, have chronic absenteeism, were retained in the previous grade level, or have various other risk factors would most likely require a tier II or tier III intervention, typically in a small group or one-on-one setting. Therefore, a mentor-mentee program designed for at-risk students would not be a tier I intervention. Research supports mentor-mentee programs as having positive impacts on student outcomes, both academic and behavioral. Mentor-mentee programs can be found both in the community and within schools. School counselors wishing to implement mentor-mentee programs could design and manage their own program or seek out a community resource for their students; regardless of where the program is managed, counselors should ensure parent permission for students to participate, especially when volunteers from the community are serving as mentors or when mentors may seek information about their mentees' progress in school.

56. D: There are a variety of ways in which a school counselor can incorporate technology into classroom guidance lessons. When making choices about technology use in classroom guidance, it is important to consider the objective of the lesson and how technology supports the objective. In this scenario, the goal was to help students learn about various careers, so a career search engine such as O*NET would provide a wide variety of information and help students discover careers they may not have previously known about. The other answer choices only help students in reference to the careers they already have knowledge of or interest in, so they do not support the objective of "increasing student knowledge of various careers."

57. C: A school counselor should not teach or assign grades for a course, especially for students on their counseling caseload. The ASCA Ethical Standards for School Counselors describe a variety of dual relationships, all of which are considered ethically inappropriate. Dual relationships that could impair the counselor's objectivity (such as counseling the child of the counselor's close personal friend) should be avoided, or mitigated if impossible to avoid. Other types of dual relationships that should be avoided include assigning grades, discipline, or acting in an administrative capacity in the absence of a school administrator.

58. C: Evaluating a student for a learning disability requires a review of a variety of existing data from a variety of sources. In addition, reviewing this data can be useful in selecting appropriate assessments for the student. For example, if a review of the child's academic record indicates a consistent difficulty in mathematics, then there is a reason to assess the child for a learning disability in mathematics. The review of existing data must be based on objective information and measurable objectives, so surveying the student would be the least appropriate.

59. B: While students may not be identified for an IEP based on their language needs, it is possible for a student who is identified as an English language learner to also have a disability that qualifies them for an IEP. Each of the other statements about ELLs is true and is an important consideration for school counselors in considering the needs of their students.

60. D: Stanines are a method of dividing a standard bell curve into nine equal statistical units, with a mean of five and a standard deviation of two. For standardized test scores, stanines are a method of comparing norm-referenced scores or percentile ranks. With a stanine comparison, scores that fall in stanines four, five, and six are considered "average" (these stanines also represent a percentile rank between 23 and 76).

61. A: In analyzing schoolwide behavior, mapping and disaggregating discipline data is an appropriate first step. Once this data is organized, the school-based team can identify the circumstances when intervention is appropriate in order to modify or support the environment in which discipline incidents are most frequent. While the other answers represent types of behavior analysis or intervention that can be appropriate in certain circumstances, mapping and disaggregating data is the most appropriate first step.

62. D: One major benefit of ASCA membership, even for school counseling students, is the availability of professional liability insurance. University field experiences offices or local school districts may add interns to their policies, but this varies widely. ASCA is the best option for Mr. Dean. The National Board for Certified Counselors is not an option for school counseling students who have not yet earned their degree.

63. D: In the examples for A and B, the counselor is consulting with the outside agency, however, the agency is acting as the consultant or expert providing information. When a school counselor is acting as a consultant, they are providing information as an expert; choice D is an example of this role. In choice C, the counselor and outside agency are working in collaboration, utilizing a team approach to develop a plan for a student.

64. A: Career counseling at the elementary level primarily focuses on exposing students to various career options and career clusters. More focused planning and research would be more appropriate at the secondary level.

65. B: Pre- and post-test data is a type of perception data that is used to measure gains in knowledge or changes in perspective. Perception data measures what people think they know, believe, or can do. Because of their subjective nature, surveys are commonly used to collect perception data, but not process or outcome data. Process data measures what a school counselor does and for whom, so subjective measures such as a survey are not applicable. Outcome data measures the impact of school counseling activities and is much more objective in nature, so this information is typically pulled from the student information system.

66. D: In any circumstance where a student requires long-term individual counseling or has significant mental health concerns beyond the scope of the school counselor's training, working with the parent (and student, if appropriate) to seek an outside mental health referral is appropriate. School counselors should not provide long-term mental health counseling in a school setting. Because nothing indicates a risk of crisis, an immediate crisis evaluation without parental permission would not be appropriate. While webinars for professional development and consultation with fellow professionals could help the counselor support the student in school, ultimately an outside referral is most appropriate for this situation due to the suspected mental health concern and need for long-term counseling.

67. B: Test reliability indicates how consistent a test is. Test validity means that the assessment measures what it is intended to measure. The SAT is a valid and reliable assessment, meaning that it measures what it is intended to measure and individual test-takers should receive the same or similar scores on repeated administrations. Individual circumstances, however, such as a recent death in the family, may mean that an individual's test score is not reliable for that administration. If that student were to repeat the test at a later date when their emotional state was not as heightened, they might perform differently.

68. B: The ASCA Mindsets & Behaviors for Student Success outlines skills and mindsets essential for student success in college and beyond. Counselors planning a classroom guidance curriculum should utilize the Mindsets & Behaviors to begin to outline learning objectives for their lessons.

69. D: Having a specific group leader is not necessary for a successful collaborative relationship. In fact, leaderless collaboration happens frequently in schools. Trust, openness, clear communication, and active listening are all necessary conditions for successful collaboration. In addition, an effective collaborative team has established norms, expectations, and a shared vision or goal. School counselors can be an asset to many collaborative teams because they are skilled in communication and active listening and can help foster trust and respect among team members.

70. C: While potential group members often do want to know who else will be in their group, disclosing the names of other group members is not part of the informed consent process. In acquiring informed consent from group members, an understanding of the purpose and goals of the group, the risks and limitations of the group, limits of confidentiality in a group setting, and training and qualifications of the counselor are all topics that should be explained to and understood by the group members. In a school setting with minors, parental consent is also necessary for informed consent.

71. D: In this scenario, the student has progressed through school-wide and classroom-wide interventions, and targeted individual intervention is appropriate. A functional behavior assessment (FBA) is a detailed method of collecting data about a student's behavior in order to develop an appropriate plan for changing inappropriate behaviors. While anecdotal evidence and historical data can be helpful, the FBA will provide the most detailed information to create an effective plan.

72. A: Answer choice A would be the best first choice in this situation. Many students respond to this kind of instructor proximity and will adjust their behavior accordingly. Other similar methods would include gently tapping on the student's work to remind them what they should be doing, or quietly whispering instructions to the students. These methods correct the behavior without embarrassing the students or giving them attention for their behavior. Answer choices B and C would not be appropriate initial strategies for low-level behavior like talking, and calling out students in public or otherwise embarrassing them often backfires. Ignoring the behavior is unlikely to result in a behavior change in this scenario.

73. C: The laissez-faire group leader generally has little participation or provides little guidance to the group; group members are generally able to make their own decisions without leader interference. Groups led by laissez-faire group leaders have a tendency to be less productive. Autocratic and authoritarian are actually two different terms for the same type of leadership style; autocratic leaders are more likely to give orders or direction to the group and expect group members to comply. Group members typically prefer this style the least. Finally, democratic leaders do provide direction and guidance for group members, but they balance that with participation in the group and input from group members. In most situations, the democratic leadership style is preferred and leads to the best outcomes for the group.

74. A: Bronfenbrenner's ecological systems theory proposed that, as children grow, the various environments (systems) in which they function interact to influence their development. Therefore, in order to understand a child's development, all of the systems must be evaluated. Bronfenbrenner proposed the following five ecological systems, ranging from the most intimate to the broadest: microsystem, mesosystem, exosystem, macrosystem, chronosystem.

75. D: ASCA has a variety of position statements that touch on academic topics, including course selection. A school counselor should use a variety of data sources when assisting with student academic planning, so using grades and standardized test data alone is not an appropriate strategy. Many school counselors may find themselves in the position where their school or district policy requires course selections to be based on grades and test scores, and in those situations, the counselor would act as an advocate for systemic change. A comprehensive school counseling program will likely use multiple strategies for facilitating course selections at any level. Grade-level meetings and/or classroom guidance lessons are very common ways to facilitate the course selection process, but counselors should keep in mind their students' background knowledge and comfort with the course selection process when opting for these strategies. In addition, students may have individual needs or specific questions that would be missed in these whole-group formats. Depending on the counselor's caseload, having individual meetings with each student and their parents may not be feasible, but there are usually individual students for whom this is appropriate.

76. A: Cognitive behavioral therapy focuses on changing irrational thoughts that lead to unwanted or negative feelings. In this scenario, the counselor would challenge the student's belief that they received a failing grade on their math test because there is something inherently wrong with them or their intelligence. Instead, the counselor may help the student reframe their difficulty, such as by saying, "I received a failing grade on my math test because I did not prepare and study effectively." Meanwhile, answer choice B would be a problem-focused approach, and choice C reflects a more solution-focused approach. Choice D represents a person-centered approach.

77. A: A focus on external punishment or consequences rather than concepts of morality is typical of seven-year-old children and is described by Kohlberg's "obedience and punishment" stage of development. The child's comment indicates the desire to avoid punishment as the main motivator for moral behavior. According to Kohlberg, most children under the age of nine are in stage 1 or stage 2 of moral development.

78. D: Holland's six basic personality types include realistic, investigative, artistic, social, enterprising, and conventional. Holland's personality theory of career counseling is based on the assumption that individuals fall into one or a combination of these six basic types. In addition, most careers or work environments correspond with these personality types, and people seek careers that allow them to express their personality type.

79. D: Teachers, along with other helping professionals such as counselors, nurses, and physical therapists, closely align with the social personality type. Examples of the other personality types include: realistic (pilot, surveyor), investigative (astronomer, physician), artistic (writer, designer), enterprising (lawyer, salesperson), and conventional (accountant, actuary).

80. B: According to Ginzberg and associates, the three stages of career development are fantasy (birth to age 11), tentative (ages 11 to 17), and realistic (ages 17 to adulthood). In this case, based on age, Sophie would be in the fantasy stage of development. Growth would be an appropriate answer choice based on Sophie's age, but that is not a stage in career development theory. Instead, growth is one of five developmental stages identified by Super.

81. A: The elementary counselor is focused on foundational social/emotional skills and academic mindsets, as well as intervention and prevention. By middle school, counselors increase the focus on positive social skills and helping students achieve their academic potential while setting future career goals. High school counselors have the strongest focus on helping students achieving academic potential and setting career goals, with additional focuses on social skills and personal growth.

82. D: There are a variety of types of career assessments depending on the approach a counselor or individual takes toward career development. Interest inventories, such as the Strong Interest Inventory, are another type of career assessment that matches an individual's interests to careers that fit those interests. Personality tests, such as the Myers-Briggs Type Indicator or Holland Code, provide an individual with information about their personality, which can be connected to careers that suit individuals with that particular personality type. Skills or aptitude assessments, such as the ASVAB, are another type of career assessment that identifies particular skills or strengths an individual has that make them well-suited to specific careers. Finally, values assessments, such as the Career Values Scale, help an individual identify the work values that are important to them. Individuals place value on different parts of their work life, such as financial success, helping others, or a low-stress work environment, which impacts the type of career or job that they will choose.

83. A: School counselors are mandated reporters, and as such, they are required to report any cases in which they suspect abuse or neglect to the appropriate social service agency. Regardless of the student's sibling stating that abuse or neglect did not occur, the student's original statements provide a reason to suspect abuse or neglect. It is not the duty of the counselor to investigate and determine if abuse or neglect did in fact occur. Each of the additional answer choices may have an appropriate place in the next steps for the student, but in cases of suspected abuse or neglect, a referral to social services is always the first step.

84. D: Criterion-referenced assessments measure the test-taker's mastery of specific skills or objectives; results can typically be expressed in terms such as "passing" or "proficient." Students taking criterion-referenced assessments have either mastered the objectives or not; the abilities of other students taking the assessment have no impact on their score or test result. Norm-referenced assessments, however, compare the individual test-taker to their peers. These results are typically expressed as a percentile rank, rather than "passing" or "proficient."

85. B: Trait-factor career counseling, based on the work of Frank Parsons, assumes that there is one best career for each individual, and that a counselor can match each individual with a single "best" career when armed with data from tests. These tests measure individual traits, including personality, in order to best match an individual with a career. Because trait-factor counseling assumes there is one "best" career for each individual, it is not considered a developmental approach. Individual changes over the lifespan, career maturity, and other developmental factors are not considered in this approach.

86. B: Despite what many schools attempt to put in place to prevent or stop bullying, research has supported the use of comprehensive, schoolwide programs over other types of bullying interventions. These types of programs aim to educate students on the types of bullying and identifying bullying behaviors, identifying different roles students play in the bullying relationship, and applying strategies for conflict resolution, assertiveness, supporting victims of bullying, and reporting bullying behaviors.

87. C: The ASCA Mindsets & Behaviors for Student Success does not discuss program evaluations or accountability, although the standards within this document can be utilized by counselors to measure student progress as part of their program evaluation. Each of the other documents explicitly discusses the requirement for counselors to conduct program evaluations. The ASCA National Model includes Accountability as one of its four components and contains a great deal of information about the evaluation process for school counseling programs. The ASCA Ethical Standards for School Counselors contains a section titled "Comprehensive Data-Informed Program" that outlines the purpose for evaluations as well as the ethical considerations in choosing and administering assessments. Finally, within the ASCA School Counselor Professional Standards & Competencies, there is a Behavior category titled "Planning and Assessment," which describes accountability-related behaviors exhibited by effective school counselors.

88. C: Consultation is an indirect service conducted on behalf of the student for the student's benefit, while individual student planning and responsive services are both examples of direct services provided directly to the student. Creating an action plan is an ASCA National Model tool based on schoolwide or subgroup data that does not involve an individual student.

89. D: Skill practice is typically not a stated goal of a support group and would not be appropriate in this situation. Skill practice would be more appropriate for an educational or therapy group.

90. C: The ABC model of cognitive behavioral therapy includes the activating event, beliefs, and consequences. The "A," or activating event, is the situation or trigger that starts the process of reacting; in this situation, the student arriving to class late and receiving a consequence were the activating events. The "B" is the belief, cognition, or thought behind the feeling or action. In this scenario, the student's belief that the consequence was unfair was the foundation of their reaction of anger. The reaction of anger is the "C," or consequence. Consequences can be emotions or behaviors, but in cognitive behavioral therapy they are always caused by beliefs or cognitions.

91. D: The program evaluation is designed to serve each of the listed purposes except for advocating for a pay raise. While school counselors advocate in general for the profession, and that may include advocating for adequate professional compensation, the individual program evaluation is not designed to serve this purpose.

92. C: The ASCA Ethical Standards for School Counselors indicate that counselors should use caution in reporting "serious and foreseeable harm." Even if the risk appears to be very low, counselors should always report threats or comments about self-harm to the students' parents. School counselors should refrain from conducting assessments for which they are not adequately trained and from making definitive statements regarding a student's risk level.

93. C: Small group counseling can be very beneficial for students with various anxiety disorders, and there are multiple programs and curricula available for counselors to use for this purpose. There are several benefits for both the students and the counselor in utilizing small group counseling for this purpose. A busy school counselor with a large caseload can see more students at one time in a small group setting, potentially increasing their effectiveness in reaching all students. Students in a group also benefit from peer exposure, learning from others' experiences, practicing new skills together, and having a level of social exposure that can help build confidence in social situations. However, group members should be carefully considered, as not all students with anxiety can immediately function in a small group setting. Some students with severe social anxiety may need preparatory individual counseling to be able to benefit from small group counseling.

94. C: This example describes collaboration, where the counselor and teacher are working together toward a common goal. Each of the other examples describes a scenario where the counselor is either providing information or gathering information to support or advocate for a student or group of students.

95. D: According to the ASCA Mindsets and Behaviors for Student Success, there are two major categories of standards relating to student development, which can be applied to all three domains of a comprehensive counseling program (academic, social/emotional, college/career). The two major categories are Mindset Standards and Behavior Standards, and Behavior Standards are further broken down into learning strategies, self-management skills, and social skills subcategories. Each of these categories of standards would be a major component of a comprehensive guidance program. Emotional regulation skills would more likely be addressed in individual or small group counseling (such as a small group focused on anger management or an individual counseling session focused on calming strategies).

96. B: Pre- and post-test data measures what participants know, believe, or can do. In this case, the pre- and post-test data specifically measures the competencies targeted during the intervention, so it would be likely to measure the effectiveness of the closing-the-gap action plan. Student surveys are another way to collect perception data, but closing-the-gap action plans specifically target a group or demographic of students, so the surveys of the whole school would not be helpful in evaluating a closing-the-gap action plan unless the data was disaggregated by subgroup. Sign-in sheets would be a method of collecting process data, and collecting this information at each portion of the intervention (such as each parent night, small group session, classroom guidance lesson, etc.) would identify data about the action plan specifically. Academic data, such as grades or achievement test results, could be an appropriate method of measuring outcome data related to an action plan, but unless the data is disaggregated by subgroup, it would not be useful in evaluating the effectiveness of the action plan.

97. B: Standardized tests pose many problems for students who are learning English as a second language. Not only do students face the difficulty of taking an assessment in a language other than their native language, but often these students struggle with cultural references within the assessments as well. For example, if a test includes a reading passage about an American holiday like the Fourth of July, students who are immigrants may not understand the references being made due to their unfamiliarity with that particular cultural experience. Therefore, even if tests are translated into a student's native language, it is still possible that the test will be invalid due to cultural references or even translation errors. Due to the vast number of languages and dialects spoken by students, it is unlikely that an assessment has been translated and validated in every language spoken by students in schools.

98. A: It is outside of the scope of the school counselor's role to provide ongoing, long-term mental health treatment; it is especially inappropriate for a school counselor to conduct this type of individual counseling with a student with significant clinical needs. Students with eating disorders are likely to need a full team of trained specialists, including a physician, nutritionist, psychiatrist, and clinical mental health counseling. Some individuals may receive these services in inpatient facilities. Each of the other roles described would be appropriate for the school counselor and would likely be beneficial for their students.

99. D: Peak physical strength is a primary characteristic of the early adulthood stage of development (approximate ages 19-45). Rapid physical growth is characteristic of both infancy (ages 0-2) and adolescence (ages 9-18). Primary sex characteristics, while present at birth, typically develop along with secondary sex characteristics during the adolescence stage.

100. D: A school counselor's skills in individual and small group counseling can certainly be a benefit to students with disabilities. However, as with all students, providing long-term individual counseling is out of the scope of appropriate responsibilities. By providing long-term individual counseling for students with IEPs, the counselor would be working outside of the scope of their training and expertise. In addition, providing this type of service to students with IEPs could lead to the school counselor only having time to provide IEP services, leaving general education students without access to the school counseling program.

101. D: Solution-focused brief therapy is, as the name implies, focused on solutions to the client's problems. Therefore, the deep analysis and exploration of the client's problems, past history, or mental health diagnosis are not necessary to begin counseling. In solution-focused brief therapy, the client is the expert, articulating their own goals and desired outcomes; the counselor is a guide who helps the client notice changes and improvements toward the desired outcome. Changes do not need to be major to be significant. The solution-focused counselor is an expert at noticing the small changes that are making a difference in progress toward the client's goal. There is a great deal of research supporting solution-focused brief counseling in a variety of client scenarios. However, a client who is unable to articulate their desired goal (such as one who has a severe intellectual disability or one who is experiencing extreme psychosis) would not be a good candidate for solution-focused brief counseling.

102. D: The ASCA Ethical Standards for School Counselors discuss confidentiality at length. While parents do have a right to information about their child, the standards described indicate that this right needs to be balanced with the confidentiality required to protect the counseling relationship.

If sensitive information does need to be shared with parents, phone calls or in-person meetings are preferred to less secure methods such as email.

103. B: Advisory councils are a part of the Manage component of the ASCA National Model and are utilized to help develop programs that are reflective of the school's needs. While students are involved in the advisory council process, it is not a direct or indirect student service under the Deliver component.

104. B: The zone of proximal development describes the concepts or skills beyond what a learner is able to do on their own, or the "zone" where the learner can accomplish a new task or skill with the help of someone else. This is a key component of Vygotsky's social development theory.

105. A: Under FERPA, students do not become "eligible students" who are granted access to their educational records until they are 18 years old or attending a post-secondary institution. Therefore, a 16-year-old would need their parents to request access to their records. Parents are permitted to inspect or request items be removed from their child's educational record at any time; even if the parent does not have physical custody of the child, they are permitted access to educational records unless a court order states otherwise. Schools are permitted to create a directory of student contact information as long as parents are given "reasonable time" to opt out of sharing directory information.

106. B: Frank Parsons was the author of *Choosing a Vocation* and the leader of the vocational counseling movement. A focus on the role of the counselor in a therapeutic role did not occur until later, with Carl Rogers' contributions to the profession. Systemic change and advocacy roles came much later, with the introduction of ASCA.

107. D: There are a great number of factors that can be addressed to help students have a successful transition to middle school. Middle school represents a huge transition for many students, with academic, personal, social, and physical changes taking place very rapidly. There are several ways both elementary and middle school counselors can work to improve outcomes for new middle schoolers, including all of the topics addressed in answer choices A, B, and C. IEP specifics would not be discussed in this type of meeting because it would not be appropriate. Students' IEP teams hold special transition meetings to address the specific needs of individual students in transitioning to the next educational level.

108. D: If an assessment is valid, it will not matter what time of day it is given. The assessment will still measure what it was intended to measure. Each of the other choices, however, may impact the ability of the test to measure what it was intended to measure. For example, altering the length of time or number of test items may allow the test-taker to complete more of the test or prevent them from completing the test. These conditions could alter the individual's score simply based on time rather than their achievement level. Explaining a test question, especially on a reading test, could impact the validity of those questions that were explained in different terms, especially if the terms in the original question were part of what was being assessed.

109. A: In this situation, the counselor is serving as the "resident expert" to provide information to the classroom teacher, who is seeking information to support his student. They are not working together to come up with a solution, which would be an example of collaboration; it is a one-way exchange of information. Consultation could be a method by which counselors provide professional development, such as by providing information to a large group of teachers. Although this consultation could result in an outside referral, as in choice D, consultation is the best description for the meeting itself in this scenario.

110. A: The mean is the average, so the average test score on this test is 50. The most common score is called the mode. Knowing the highest possible test score is useful in determining the range, which is the highest score minus the lowest score. The percentage of students who passed the test is useful information for instructional or curricular decisions and is called a passing rate or proficiency rate (usually with standardized end-of-grade tests).

111. B: When it comes to providing equal access to the curriculum via a Section 504 plan or IEP, the most common terms used are "accommodation" and "modification." While counselors will frequently hear and use these terms in conjunction with each other, they refer to different types of strategies. Accommodations are those strategies that change the environment, time, type of output, or size of the task at hand without fundamentally changing the task, instructional level, or content that the student is learning. Accommodations allow students to access the curriculum as well as their non-disabled peers and perform the same learning tasks as their peers. Preferential seating (such as seating away from distractions or close to the teacher) is an example of environmental accommodation. Extended time is an accommodation that changes the length of time given to complete a task without changing the task itself. Modifications, however, change the task or content itself based on a child's needs. Modifications may lower or change the learning standards expected of the student. An example of a modification would be giving a child an alternative reading passage on their reading level. Interventions are instructional strategies used to help a child learn content; an example would be small group instruction.

112. B: Trauma-informed practices would be the most reasonable place for this counselor to start when working with this family. The children experienced a traumatic event and are demonstrating classic effects of trauma. Family systems therapy would be conducted in a mental health setting with a trained therapist. Multi-tiered systems of support and positive behavior intervention and support may be somewhat helpful for the children, but trauma-informed practices are the best support for recovery from a traumatic experience.

113. A: Advisory councils are recommended to meet at least twice per year, but they are certainly not required to meet quarterly. No matter the frequency, the advisory council should utilize an agenda and meeting minutes to keep the meetings on track. Advisory councils can assist school counselors with a variety of tasks, including advising on program goals, reviewing program results, making recommendations for future program goals, and advocating for the school counseling program. School counselors are encouraged to recruit a diverse group of stakeholders to participate in an advisory council, and the recommended size is 8–20 members.

114. A: The ASCA National Model states the question to be answered by the program evaluation as "How are students different as a result of the school counseling program?" Within the program evaluation, data about academic achievement, progress toward stated goals and objectives, counselor use of time, and the effectiveness of program components is collected and evaluated, but the impact on students is the focus of the evaluation process. Measuring student impact allows the school counselor to understand their progress toward stated goals and to identify areas for improvement or adjustments to their counseling program.

115. A: In prescriptive mode, consultants (school counselors) provide plans based on their knowledge of a situation. In other words, they prescribe a solution. In mediation mode, school counselors may work with two parties who need assistance resolving a dispute, and the counselor may offer solutions for resolving the dispute. In provision mode, the consultant may step into the scenario to carry out the suggested plan or strategy. For example, the counselor may go into the classroom to carry out the strategies suggested. Finally, initiation mode is when the consultant may recognize that supports or strategies are needed without the third party requesting that support, and come in to offer assistance. For example, the counselor notices a student is struggling and steps in to offer solutions.

116. A: The ASCA Ethical Standards are clear when it comes to dual relationships. In this case, by providing individual counseling to a teacher, Mrs. Harris puts herself in a situation where she is creating a dual relationship that could negatively impact students. For example, if a student comes in later to discuss the problems they are having in that teacher's class, it would be difficult for Mrs. Harris to remain neutral because she has been providing individual counseling regarding personal concerns with the same teacher. The teacher's mental health indeed impacts students, but providing mental health counseling to the teacher is beyond the scope of the school counselor's role. Of course, Mrs. Harris should still maintain confidentiality regarding the teacher's concerns and should not approach HR on behalf of the teacher.

117. C: Standardized achievement tests measure an individual's skill or knowledge in a specific subject area. In this case, the test was designed to measure the student's mastery of grade-level skills and concepts in math. The student's score of "not proficient" indicates that the student did not demonstrate mastery of all of these skills. This may be a result of the instruction the student received. However, it should not be interpreted as a demonstration of low, or comparatively lower, intelligence.

118. A: The annual agreement is a document signed by both the school counselor and their administrator after a formal conversation about the focus and goals of the counseling program for the upcoming year. It is a crucial piece of the Management component, especially in identifying priorities for the upcoming year and discussing appropriate and inappropriate duties. Each of the other answer choices does describe a tool or product from the Management component, but the goals and outcomes from each are different than an annual agreement. The advisory council provides the school counselor with feedback and advice on the overall school counseling program, while the annual calendar outlines program priorities and publishes program activities for stakeholders, and the curriculum plan outlines the classroom guidance curriculum and aligned student standards.

119. C: Primarily, the school counselor's role in educating students with disabilities has to do with advocating for their students' rights. While the counselor's role in school-based teams will vary between schools and districts, ASCA states that school counselors should not lead or supervise writing or implementing plans under IDEA or Section 504. Even with an IEP or Section 504 plan, it is always inappropriate for school counselors to provide long-term counseling to students.

120. C: There are multiple factors to consider in this scenario to ensure students and parents have the level of support needed: the rural location, length of commute to the school, and lack of experience with college processes in both the students and parents. A live and recorded version of the workshop provides multiple pathways for parents, including working parents or those who live far from school, to access the instruction needed to complete the FAFSA. Choices B and D do not provide parents without college experience the support needed to complete the FAFSA successfully and choice A relies on students to relay complex information to their parents.

Practice Test #2

1. Which major component of a comprehensive school counseling program most directly allows a school counselor to demonstrate school-level leadership?

a. Counseling curriculum
b. Individual student planning
c. Responsive services
d. System support

2. The ASCA Mindsets & Behaviors for Student Success outlines standards or student learning that can be addressed through a classroom guidance curriculum. Which of the four components of the ASCA National Model Program includes these standards?

a. Define
b. Manage
c. Deliver
d. Assess

3. Which of the following is an example of a technique specifically used in solution-focused brief counseling?

a. Scaling questions
b. Free association
c. Changing self-talk
d. Empty chair

4. Mr. Matthews, a high school counselor, is participating in an IEP team meeting for Rachel, a student with a learning disability. Rachel's parents have many requests for modifications and accommodations in her IEP, some of which the teachers have told Mr. Matthews privately they feel are "unreasonable." Mr. Matthews is trying to help the two groups communicate about what is best for Rachel and serve as an advocate for her needs, but he also knows one of Rachel's parents' requests is not permitted under IDEA. Which of the following requests would NOT be required of the school under IDEA?

a. Accommodations, such as extended time on tests
b. Preferential treatment in athletic tryouts
c. Education in the regular education classroom
d. Specially designed instruction

5. A middle school counselor is planning an anti-bullying curriculum for classroom guidance lessons. Which of the following statements is NOT true about middle school students and bullying?

a. Middle school girls are more likely to experience social bullying than physical bullying.
b. Middle school students are likely to experience or participate in cyberbullying.
c. Middle school students who are "bystanders" are encouraging bullying to continue.
d. Middle school boys and girls experience and participate in social bullying to equal degrees.

6. According to the ASCA National Model, which of the following would be the most appropriate role for school counselors in dealing with bullying?

a. Issuing discipline for students who bully others
b. Changing schedules for students who are victims of bullying so they feel safe
c. Participating in the planning of a comprehensive, schoolwide anti-bullying program
d. Investigating complaints of bullying in order to recommend consequences

7. Ms. Howell is a first-year counselor at an elementary school. In preparation for the upcoming school year, she works with her building principal to articulate how the school counseling program aligns with the school/district mission and vision.

This work most closely aligns with which component of the ASCA National Model (Fifth Edition)?

a. Define
b. Manage
c. Deliver
d. Assess

8. Which of the following school counselor roles is NOT appropriate in supporting school administration?

a. Providing counseling to students who have disciplinary problems
b. Helping the principal identify and resolve student issues
c. Advocating for students at student support team meetings
d. Performing disciplinary actions, such as issuing consequences

9. Carl Rogers' person-centered therapy identifies three key factors necessary for an effective helping relationship. Which of the following is NOT one of these key factors?

a. Congruence
b. Unconditional positive regard
c. Empathy
d. Transference

10. Kevin, a high school student, completes the Strong Interest Inventory as part of a classroom guidance lesson. The results indicate that Kevin has a strong Social type. Which of the following would be an appropriate use of this assessment result?

a. The counselor shows Kevin how to use a career database to learn more about careers in the Social category.
b. The counselor discourages Kevin from taking computer science electives because they do not fit his Social personality type.
c. The counselor registers Kevin for public speaking classes to develop his social skills.
d. The counselor encourages Kevin to join a small group counseling session focused on social skills.

11. A school counselor conducts a needs assessment with students and staff. Using the data gathered from the needs assessment, the counselor could do all of the following EXCEPT:

a. Identify small-group counseling topics
b. Design classroom guidance curriculum
c. Identify individual student needs
d. Evaluate the previous year's program

12. Which of the following is an example of consultation?

a. Two school counselors work together to plan a schoolwide classroom guidance curriculum.
b. A school counselor and principal meet to sign an annual agreement before the school year starts.
c. A school counselor meets with the school's speech therapist to learn about strategies to support a student who stutters.
d. A school counselor participates in an IEP team meeting to determine appropriate services for a student with a learning disability.

13. A school counselor is reviewing data and finds that the school's graduation rate improved from 73% to 79% over the course of two school years. Which type of data is this?

a. Activity evaluation data
b. Competency attainment data
c. Achievement outcome data
d. Subgroup achievement data

14. James is a middle school student in a counseling group. During a group session, the school counselor notices that James has been more withdrawn and has not been participating in the group discussion. Which of the following strategies would be an appropriate response to this observation?

a. Ignore James's non-participation, as group participation is voluntary.
b. Pull James aside during the group session and have a conversation with him about his participation.
c. Make a connection between James and another group member.
d. Remove James from the group, as his non-participation is threatening other group members' progress.

15. Ms. Gilmore is entering her second year as a high school counselor. During a collaborative meeting with her building principal to discuss the annual agreement for the upcoming school year, Ms. Gilmore reviews the tasks and activities that have been assigned to her. Which of the following activities would Ms. Gilmore advocate to have reassigned, as it is NOT appropriate for a school counselor?

a. Providing core classroom guidance curriculum
b. Counseling students about appropriate dress for school
c. Calculating grade point averages for students
d. Ensuring student records are maintained according to state and federal regulations

16. Which of the following would be an appropriate role for an elementary school counselor in regard to kindergarten readiness?

a. Administering kindergarten entry assessments
b. Processing kindergarten enrollments
c. Conducting early kindergarten entry assessments
d. Collaborating with teachers to plan for transitional support

17. A school counselor implements a classroom guidance program aimed at improving graduation rates. During the annual program evaluation, the counselor analyzes a variety of data to determine the effectiveness of the program and implement changes for the following year. Which of the following pieces of data gathered by the counselor represents perception data?

a. 450 students in grades 9-12 completed three classroom lessons with their counselor.
b. 120 9th-grade students submitted complete four-year graduation plans to their counselor.
c. 135 students indicated they feel "very prepared" to complete high school in four years.
d. The school's current four-year graduation rate is 83%, an increase of 7% over last year.

18. Which of the following school counselor roles is NOT appropriate in relation to standardized testing?

a. Disaggregating test results in order to drive instructional and programming decisions
b. Providing classroom guidance for students designed to reduce test anxiety
c. Coordinating the school's testing program, including accommodations for students with disabilities
d. Advocating for standardized tests to be culturally and linguistically unbiased

19. The purpose of an interest inventory, such as the Strong Interest Inventory, is best described as which of the following?

a. To help an individual learn about how their personality impacts their interests
b. To help an individual match their interests with potential careers
c. To help an individual develop new interests, such as hobbies or activities
d. To help an individual understand how they relate to others

20. An educational trend that directly impacts the role of school counselors is the multi-tiered systems of support (MTSS) framework. Which of the following describes an appropriate role for school counselors in implementing MTSS?

a. Coordinating referrals for students into the intervention process as well as maintaining appropriate data collection
b. Coordinating standardized testing programs in order to help identify appropriate interventions
c. Providing standards-based academic, social/emotional, and career curriculum to all students
d. Providing individual counseling to all students identified as tier III students

21. One of the essential roles of a school counselor is consultation. Consultation is considered which type of service?

a. Responsive service
b. Individual student planning
c. School counseling core curriculum
d. Indirect student service

22. Ms. Brown is facing an ethical dilemma regarding the expectations of her principal when it comes to student confidentiality. Her principal feels there is a legitimate educational need for the counselor to breach student confidentiality and share information from individual counseling sessions. Which of the following is the best course of action for Ms. Brown?

a. Ms. Brown should adhere to the expectations of her principal, who is her direct supervisor.
b. Ms. Brown should always uphold the confidentiality of her student, regardless of her principal's concerns.
c. Ms. Brown should consult both the ASCA guidelines and state law for guidance.
d. Ms. Brown should share the information with the student's parents so they can discuss it with the principal.

23. A school counselor completes a school data profile in order to plan their school counseling program. In analyzing the data gathered, the counselor notes that the school's graduation rate has gradually decreased over the last few years among students with disabilities. Based on the available data, what ASCA National Model document should the counselor use to address this concern?

a. Curriculum action plan
b. Small group action plan
c. Closing-the-gap action plan
d. Lesson plan

Refer to the following for question 24:

> A middle school counselor analyzes attendance data and finds that, in a specific classroom, all but six students have attendance rates above 90%. These six students are failing several classes, mostly due to incomplete assignments, missing homework, and late projects. The teacher has contacted the students' parents but has not tried anything else to address these problems.

24. Which of the following interventions would be appropriate in this scenario?

a. Holding a parent information night about grading policies and course requirements
b. Conducting a classroom guidance lesson about how to calculate class averages and the impact of individual assignments
c. Initiating a special education referral for each of the six students to evaluate for executive functioning deficits or learning disabilities
d. Conducting a small group focused on academic skills, such as time management and organizing assignments

25. Which of the following statements is true regarding electronic communications according to the ASCA Ethical Standards for School Counselors?

a. Electronic communication between the school counselor and other individuals represents a form of privileged communication and is confidential.
b. Electronic communication between school officials about an individual student can create an official school record under FERPA.
c. Electronic communication about an individual student does not create an official school record under FERPA as long as the student's name is not used.
d. The only form of electronic communication that constitutes an official school record is that which takes place within the official student information system (SIS).

26. Ms. Taylor is a school counselor who is working with a family that is new to her school. The children do not have documents such as social security cards and Ms. Taylor suspects that the children are undocumented immigrants. What is Ms. Taylor's ethical obligation regarding her students' rights in this situation?

a. Ms. Taylor should call her local immigration office to report the family's undocumented status.
b. Ms. Taylor should refer the family to an immigration attorney to help them seek legal status.
c. Ms. Taylor should ensure that the students' records accurately reflect their immigration status.
d. Ms. Taylor should advocate for the students to have equal access to all school programs.

27. Which of the following student differences would NOT be a likely cause of cultural bias on a test?

a. Differences in English proficiency
b. Differences in socioeconomic status
c. Differences in classroom grouping
d. Differences in gender

28. Classroom guidance is most often considered to be which type of counseling activity?

a. Prevention
b. Intervention
c. Outreach
d. Academic

29. A test is considered standardized when certain components of the test and testing environment are the same among test-takers. In order for a test to be standardized, all of the following components are required to be the same EXCEPT:

a. The length of time given to take the test
b. The age of the individuals taking the test
c. The number of questions on the test
d. The instructions given when taking the test

30. A school counselor receives a signed request from an outside clinical mental health agency for information about a student they are treating, including their grades and attendance record. How should the counselor respond?

a. Ignore the request because sharing this type of information is not legal
b. Call the agency to discuss their request and their work with the student
c. Forward a copy of the request to the data clerk to process copies of the child's records
d. Seek written consent from the student's parents to share information with the agency

31. Which of the following is NOT an appropriate use of end-of-grade standardized test scores?

a. Identifying an individual student's academic strengths
b. Improving classroom instructional plans
c. Determining eligibility for special education services
d. Tracking an individual student's academic growth

32. Which of the following is NOT a type of results report completed as part of a school counseling program evaluation?

a. Curriculum results report
b. Individual results report
c. Small-group results report
d. Closing-the-gap results report

33. Which of the following is NOT an appropriate method by which a school counselor would support students with disabilities under IDEA?

a. Providing classroom guidance curriculum to students with special needs as part of the full school program
b. Encouraging a student's parents to participate in a scheduled IEP meeting
c. Writing social-emotional goals for a student's IEP to be addressed through counseling
d. Providing short-term, goal-focused individual counseling as part of a student's IEP

34. In which of the following scenarios would student work samples NOT be an appropriate data source for evaluation?

a. Measuring the impact of instructional interventions
b. Understanding a child's proficiency in the English language
c. Evaluating a student for autism spectrum disorder
d. Evaluating a student's mastery of academic standards

35. A school counselor who recently completed an annual program evaluation is planning how they will share their results. Which of the following methods for sharing program results is least likely to achieve the goals outlined by ASCA for sharing results?

a. Printing a hard copy of the results report to keep in the counseling office
b. Presenting the results report to the school board and administration
c. Including the results report on the counseling department website
d. Sharing the results report with the counseling advisory committee

36. In which of the following scenarios would observation of a student by a counselor or other professional be an appropriate method of gathering data?

a. Evaluating if a child has an attention-related disability such as ADHD
b. Assessing the effectiveness of instructional interventions
c. Tracking the frequency of a behavior targeted in a behavior intervention plan
d. Determining if a child requires special education services

37. A school counselor wishes to collect process data about their counseling program activities in order to effectively evaluate their programming. Which of the following methods of data collection would produce this type of data?

a. Collecting student feedback on classroom guidance lessons via survey
b. Calculating student grade point averages and disaggregating them by grade level
c. Having students complete pre- and post-tests after each classroom guidance lesson
d. Having parents sign in on an attendance sheet at a parent information night

38. A school counselor shares strategies that will support an individual student's achievement with that student's parents and teachers. Which of the following school counselor activities is this?

a. Consulting
b. Collaborating
c. Evaluating
d. Counseling

39. A school counselor is working with a student, Annie, whose anxiety about school performance has been interfering with her ability to function in the classroom. The counselor is applying cognitive behavioral techniques in individual counseling with the student. Which of the following represents an appropriate outcome goal for this scenario?

a. Annie will develop academic skills to use in the classroom.
b. Annie will learn to change her thinking and self-talk about school.
c. Annie will build trust with the counselor to talk about her struggles in school.
d. Annie will receive accommodations from her classroom teacher to support her.

40. Mr. Golden is a school counselor whose religious beliefs discourage same-sex relationships. A student shares in individual counseling that he is in a same-sex relationship. What is Mr. Golden's ethical obligation in working with this student?

a. Mr. Golden should refer the student to a different counselor within the school due to the bias his religious beliefs create.
b. Mr. Golden should share his bias with the student so that the student has a full understanding before giving informed consent.
c. Mr. Golden should seek training and development in this area to help him provide comprehensive services to the student.
d. Mr. Golden should terminate the counseling relationship with the student, as his beliefs are constitutionally protected.

41. Which of the following school counselor activities is most directly related to Title II of the Education Amendments of 1976?

a. A school counselor conducts classroom guidance lessons on sexual harassment prevention to all students in a middle school.
b. A school counselor analyzes career-focused classroom guidance curricula to select one that reduces gender bias in career guidance.
c. A school counselor advocates for the right of a student with ADHD to access the curriculum as equally as his non-disabled peers.
d. A school counselor advises a parent of their right to inspect their child's educational record and request that certain items be removed.

42. A state requires all of its students to take an assessment each year that measures mastery of grade-level content standards taught during the year. This type of assessment is best described as which of the following?

a. Achievement test
b. Aptitude test
c. Placement test
d. Norm-referenced test

43. Mrs. Martin, a school counselor, is analyzing data about her school counseling program to identify areas for program improvement. She is reviewing perception data from a series of classroom guidance lessons delivered to 5th graders. Which of the following questions could be answered by analyzing this data?

a. Did all students receive the same curriculum?
b. What impact did the lessons have on student GPAs?
c. Did the pre- and post-tests indicate an increase in knowledge related to the lesson objectives?
d. Were the lessons delivered as planned?

44. A school utilizes a reward system in which students can exchange tickets for small prizes. A student at the school has been demonstrating the behavior of blurting out answers instead of raising his hand. When he raises his hand before blurting out an answer, his teacher gives him a ticket for a prize. According to B.F. Skinner's operant conditioning theory, the ticket represents which type of consequence?

a. Positive reinforcement
b. Negative reinforcement
c. Punishment
d. Neutral consequence

45. Riley is a 7th-grade student who reports to her school counselor that some boys in her class repeatedly send inappropriate photos to her via text message and then ask her about the photos during school. Riley is embarrassed and uncomfortable with this type of message and the resulting attention at school. What is Riley's counselor's best course of action in this scenario?

a. The counselor should tell Riley to ignore the comments and block the messages but cannot pursue any further action because text messages are protected speech.
b. The counselor should tell Riley to report the situation to her teacher because that is the first person who should be intervening, according to the school's harassment policy.
c. The counselor should collaborate with administration to correct the behavior because the boys are creating a hostile environment for Riley.
d. The counselor should help Riley practice standing up to the boys because this is the only way the behavior will stop.

46. According to the ASCA National Model, which of the following tasks related to assisting students with post-secondary plans is an appropriate activity for a school counselor?

a. Calculating class rank and grade point average
b. Coordinating schoolwide SAT testing
c. Assisting students with understanding course selections
d. Copying records needed for college applications

47. A school counselor is conducting student training for a peer mediation program. She is writing role-play scripts for students to act out various types of communication strategies they may use in the peer mediation process. Which of the following script phrases represents a communication approach or technique that she would NOT want her students to practice using in the peer mediation process?

a. "I think you should..."
b. "Can you tell me more?"
c. "What I hear you saying is…"
d. "I can see why you feel that way."

48. In designing and implementing a comprehensive school counseling program, which of the following is NOT a type of action plan utilized by the ASCA National Model?

a. Curriculum action plan
b. Small-group action plan
c. Closing-the-gap action plan
d. Use-of-time action plan

49. Which of the following is NOT an appropriate academic advising activity for a school counselor?

a. Interpreting achievement tests
b. Keeping academic records
c. Interpreting student records
d. Analyzing grades in relation to achievement

50. A school counselor is developing a list of community agencies for referrals for the upcoming school year. Which of the following is NOT a step the counselor should take in developing this list?

a. Contact each agency to determine if they are open and accepting new referrals.
b. Submit the list to the school or district for vetting and approval according to policy.
c. Make a list of the agencies current students and families utilize for counseling.
d. Gather information about the services each agency provides, including whether they accept insurance.

51. Ms. Joseph, a school counselor, has been working with an anxious student individually for several weeks. It is clear that the child's needs are significant and the anxiety is interfering with his ability to attend school. Ms. Joseph recognizes that her training is not adequate for the needs of the student. What is Ms. Joseph's ethical obligation in this scenario?

a. Ms. Joseph should seek additional training and development in this area in order to better support the student.
b. Ms. Joseph should refer the child's parents to a counselor she knows who has been effective with other anxious students in the past.
c. Ms. Joseph should stop seeing the child and tell his parents that he should see an outside counselor.
d. Ms. Joseph should provide the child's parents with a list of referrals and continue working with the child in the meantime.

52. Which of the following types of assessments is best used to measure a student's mastery of concepts taught in a specific course?

a. Formative assessment
b. Diagnostic assessment
c. Summative assessment
d. Norm-referenced assessment

53. Which of the following is an appropriate use of intelligence assessments, such as the WISC, in a school setting?

a. As a component of a psycho-educational evaluation
b. As the sole determinant of eligibility for special education services
c. To guide students toward appropriate career paths
d. To make placement decisions for honors coursework

54. Which of the following is NOT true about the ASCA Mindsets & Behaviors for Student Success?

a. The Mindsets & Behaviors include 36 standards that students should be able to demonstrate as the result of a comprehensive school counseling program.
b. The Mindsets & Behaviors are aligned to the ASCA National Standards for Students and are delineated by grade-level competencies.
c. The Mindsets & Behaviors can be aligned to Common Core or other state standards by grade-level competencies.
d. Each of the Mindsets & Behaviors can be applied to all three domains (academic, social/emotional, career).

55. A student who has been diagnosed with ADHD is demonstrating difficulty on standardized reading assessments due to her disability. Her school counselor is working with the Section 504 team to develop a plan for the student, including testing accommodations. Which of the following would NOT be an appropriate accommodation in this scenario?

a. Providing extended time to complete assessments
b. Having a test administrator read the assessments aloud
c. Providing frequent breaks during assessments
d. Eliminating the use of bubble sheets during assessments

56. Janice is a seventh-grade student who was referred to the counselor after making a comment in class about wanting to "kill herself." In the conversation with the school counselor, Janice says that she was not serious about being suicidal and just making an off-hand comment and asks the counselor to "not make a big deal about it." The counselor believes Janice's explanation. What is the school counselor's ethical responsibility in this scenario?

a. The counselor has a duty to warn the parent of Janice's threat of harm, regardless of her intent.
b. The counselor has a responsibility to maintain Janice's confidentiality and keep their conversation private.
c. The counselor has a responsibility to conduct a formal assessment to determine Janice's level of risk before proceeding.
d. The counselor has a responsibility to create a safety plan with Janice to ensure she does not harm herself.

57. A school counselor has been working with a student, Joey, who was previously diagnosed with depression. The counselor has had four individual sessions with Joey, who has not reported any progress or improvement in his depression. The strategies the counselor has tried with Joey have not been successful. Which of the following steps should the counselor consider next?

a. Provide Joey's parents with a list of referrals for outside mental health counseling.
b. Seek additional training on counseling strategies for students with depression.
c. Refer Joey to the school nurse to rule out physical causes for his symptoms.
d. Invite Joey to join a small group counseling session focused on self-esteem.

58. A school counselor is planning a classroom guidance lesson on career development. Based on psychological career theory, what would be an appropriate first activity to include in this lesson?

a. Having students research careers they are already interested in
b. Having students complete a survey to determine their personality type
c. Taking a field trip to visit a real-life work setting
d. Having students research the skills and abilities needed for various careers

59. A school counselor plans to advocate with their school district for an appropriate counselor-to-student ratio. Which of the following would be the most appropriate and effective data source to support their request?

a. Counselor use-of-time assessment
b. ASCA research publications
c. Counseling program annual calendar
d. Recognized ASCA Model Program

60. In a private conversation with the school counselor, Mr. Morris, a high school teacher, said that he is concerned about bullying by students in his classroom. He reports that several students have been making comments about a student, Sally, during independent work, and refusing to allow her to join them during group work. Sally has been visibly upset after these interactions but has not made any complaints to Mr. Morris or other teachers. What should the school counselor do next?

a. Talk to the principal about the need to support Mr. Morris's classroom management.
b. Wait for Sally to make a report or complaint of bullying.
c. Ask Sally to come talk to the counselor in their office.
d. File a formal bullying complaint with the principal.

61. Which stage of the group counseling process represents the majority of the group's time?

a. Initial/forming
b. Transition/storming
c. Working/norming
d. Termination/adjourning

62. The counseling theory focusing on feelings of inferiority vs. superiority and the birth order of the client is based on whose work?

a. Erik Erikson
b. Alfred Adler
c. Sigmund Freud
d. Erich Fromm

63. Brianna is a 3rd-grade student whose teacher reports that she regularly interrupts classroom instruction by getting up out of her seat and "wandering around the room." Which of the following methods for collecting data would provide the most useful information for creating an intervention for Brianna?

a. A tally sheet to record the number of times the behavior occurs in a day
b. A functional behavior assessment to determine the function of the behavior
c. A checklist to record the number of times the behavior occurs and in which situations
d. An observation by a staff member to take notes about the behavior

64. Mrs. Bell is a middle school counselor who is a part of her school's intervention team. The team is reviewing intervention data for a group of students who were retained in their previous grade and are completing their second year in the same grade placement. The team has determined that five students from this group need a tier II intervention. Which of the following describes an example of a tier II intervention?

a. Quality, research-based instruction provided in the regular classroom
b. Referring each of the five students for a special education evaluation
c. Classroom guidance lessons focused on student skills
d. Small group instruction focused on skill deficits

65. On which of the components of a comprehensive school counseling program should a counselor ideally spend the majority of their time?

a. Define
b. Manage
c. Deliver
d. Assess

66. The school data profile is a spreadsheet template that school counselors can utilize to track which of the following data points?

a. Disaggregated achievement data
b. Attainment of competencies data
c. Counseling process data
d. Needs assessment data

67. Grace is a high school student who asks her school counselor for support in choosing a career path. Using Frank Parsons' career counseling approach, what would be the first step Grace's counselor should take in beginning the career counseling process?

a. Having a conversation with Grace about her goals, interests, aspirations, and personality
b. Having Grace complete several tests in order to collect data about her personal traits
c. Having Grace research careers that interest her to identify possibilities
d. Having Grace complete the Self-Directed Search to determine her personality type

68. Which of the following is true regarding the rights of students and parents?

a. A counselor's primary obligation is to protect the student's right to confidentiality, but this right must be balanced with the parent's right to make decisions on their child's behalf.
b. A counselor's primary obligation is to protect the student's right to confidentiality, even if that is at odds with a parent's right to make decisions on their child's behalf.
c. A counselor's obligation to protect the student's right to confidentiality and the parent's right to make decisions on their child's behalf are equal.
d. A counselor's primary obligation is to protect the parent's right to make decisions on their child's behalf, as minor children do not have the right to confidentiality.

69. Which of the following statements is NOT true about percentile rank as it pertains to standardized test scores?

a. The percentile rank reflects an individual's performance compared to a norm-referenced group.
b. The percentile rank reflects the percent of test questions answered correctly on a norm-referenced test.
c. The percentile rank can also be described as the percentage of one's peers that an individual equals or surpasses in performance.
d. A percentile rank between the 23rd and 76th percentile is considered "average."

70. A school counselor is leading a counseling group focused on developing study skills. During a particular session, the counselor encourages self-disclosure and points out similarities between group members. What is the counselor's goal in these types of comments?

a. Allaying anxiety
b. Establishing cohesion
c. Protecting the welfare of the individual
d. Establishing trust

71. Hanna is a new kindergarten student who is legally blind. Her parents talk to the school counselor during the enrollment process and ask for information about the services and supports their daughter will be able to access in school. Which of the following laws or programs would the counselor refer to in order to provide guidance about Hanna's situation?

a. IDEA
b. Section 504
c. FERPA
d. ESSA

72. A school counselor working to create an academic intervention plan for a student is most likely to utilize which of the following approaches to develop the plan?

a. Strengths-based focus
b. Problem identification
c. Cognitive behavioral therapy
d. Family therapy

73. Jane's father drops by the school counselor's office to discuss his difficulties getting Jane to complete her homework. The school counselor asks Jane's father to tell her more about what is happening at home, including times when Jane has completed her homework successfully and what strategies have worked in their household in the past. The school counselor discusses strategies that have worked for other students in similar situations, and she and Jane's father create a plan for the following week. Which of the following school counselor roles is best described by this scenario?

a. Consulting
b. Collaborating
c. Evaluating
d. Counseling

74. An individual has begun to compare their accomplishments to those of their peers and feels a sense of pride in how they compare to others. According to Erik Erikson, this individual is in which stage of development?

a. Autonomy vs. shame (ages 2–3)
b. Initiative vs. guilt (ages 3–6)
c. Industry vs. inferiority (ages 6–12)
d. Identity vs. role confusion (ages 12–18)

75. A school counselor is creating a spreadsheet of student achievement data that includes end-of-grade test scores, graduation rates, and enrollment in honors courses. The counselor disaggregates the data by student subgroup. The counselor is most likely compiling this data for which of the following tasks?

a. Creating a closing-the-gap action plan
b. Creating a small-group action plan
c. Preparing the annual agreement
d. Conducting a needs assessment

76. An elementary school has two school counselors. They each maintain their own caseload for classroom guidance, individual counseling, and small groups. Each year, the two counselors plan and implement a schoolwide career day, sharing equally in the planning and other tasks. Which of the following school counselor roles are the counselors demonstrating in the planning of career day?

a. Consulting
b. Collaborating
c. Evaluating
d. Counseling

77. What is one reason a counselor might use an online college search with students?

a. To ensure students only apply to colleges for which they have a high chance of admission
b. To provide students with a wide knowledge base about various colleges
c. To eliminate the need for face-to-face individual student planning with the counselor
d. To ensure all students apply to colleges that they can afford without financial aid

78. Mr. Preston is conducting a conflict resolution session between two 3rd-grade boys after an altercation at recess. Sam is upset because he wanted to play soccer with a group of boys, and Kyle told him he couldn't play. Kyle was the team captain, so the other boys went along with what he said, and Sam wasn't able to join the game. Sam feels left out and sad; Kyle says that he likes playing with Sam, but Sam is not a good soccer player and would have made his team lose. Which of the following possible resolutions represents a collaborative outcome?

a. Sam agrees to do something else at recess so that Kyle's team won't lose the game.
b. Kyle agrees to play a different game at recess so that Sam won't feel left out.
c. Kyle agrees to only play soccer every other day, alternating with a different game that Sam can play.
d. Kyle and Sam agree to practice soccer skills together so that Sam improves and they can play together.

Refer to the following for questions 79–80:

> Anthony is a 5th-grade student who struggles with focus and attention in the classroom. He has been getting poor grades on assessments and classwork for several months, complaining of headaches, and demonstrating a short attention span in class. His teacher has come to the counselor because she doesn't know how to help Anthony. He does not have a formal diagnosis of ADHD.

79. Which of the following would be an appropriate first step for the counselor to take in supporting Anthony?

a. The counselor should provide individual counseling to Anthony to improve his focus and attention.
b. The counselor should contact Anthony's parents to have them submit a written request for a special education evaluation.
c. The counselor should help the teacher identify areas of concern and work with the teacher to address those areas according to the school's intervention process.
d. The counselor should refer Anthony to the appropriate team for a special education evaluation.

80. Which of the following would be an appropriate internal referral for the student described?

a. The school psychologist for a psycho-educational evaluation
b. The school nurse for a vision screening
c. The exceptional children's division for a full evaluation
d. The school social worker for suspicion of abuse or neglect

81. Which of the following is true regarding the implementation of ASCA Mindsets and Behaviors for Student Success?

a. They replaced the previous academic, career, and social/emotional domains.
b. They differ at each school level (elementary, middle, and high school).
c. They are designed to be delivered through classroom guidance.
d. They can be aligned to school and district goals across domains and grade levels.

82. A school counselor is designing a mentoring program for students at school and is compiling information about school-based mentor programs to present to the principal. Based on available research, which of the following results would NOT be expected to be a possible outcome of a school-based mentoring program?

a. Increased executive functioning skills
b. Increased academic performance for mentees
c. Reduction of academic achievement gap
d. Reduction in truancy rates for mentees

83. Mrs. Black is holding the first of six group counseling sessions. Which of the following is NOT an appropriate goal for this stage of the group counseling process?

a. Explaining the purpose of the group
b. Establishing behavioral and confidentiality expectations for group members
c. Encouraging the development of group cohesion
d. Addressing conflict between group members

Refer to the following for question 84:

Mrs. Johnson is a middle school counselor who has been working with a seventh-grade student in individual counseling. The student was diagnosed by an outside therapist with an anxiety disorder and regularly earns failing grades on tests despite excellent classwork and homework grades. Mrs. Johnson convenes a team meeting to discuss appropriate accommodations for the student under Section 504. Since she has other students that also struggle with anxiety disorders, she is also considering adding the student to a small counseling group.

84. Which role of the school counselor was Mrs. Johnson primarily demonstrating in this situation?

a. Advocate
b. Collaborator
c. Leader
d. Consultant

85. Amy, a high school student, is in crisis. The school counselor is called because Amy is crying uncontrollably in the hallway, making statements about wanting to harm herself. Amy seems visibly calmer after talking with the counselor, but she continues to make concerning statements about wanting to kill herself, indicating that she has a firm plan to carry out an attempt to kill herself that weekend. Assuming each possibility is compliant with school and district policies, what is the appropriate next step for the school counselor to take?

a. Contact Amy's parents to pick her up and encourage them to set up an appointment with a therapist.
b. Call Child Protective Services to conduct an investigation and ensure that Amy is safe at home.
c. Call the local mental health urgent care or crisis response unit to conduct a crisis evaluation.
d. Have Amy sign a no-harm contract, promising not to harm herself and outlining steps she should take if she has suicidal thoughts.

86. A young student (age 5) does not yet understand that liquid poured from a short, wide glass maintains the same volume when poured into a tall, narrow glass. His older sibling (age 9) understands that the liquid retains the same volume in both containers. Which concept of Piaget's theory of cognitive development is demonstrated by this scenario?

a. Assimilation
b. Accommodation
c. Conservation
d. Classification

87. Kelly is a second-grade student who demonstrates distractibility, forgetfulness, and task avoidance at school. He struggles to complete tasks, organize his materials, and frequently loses items needed for school. His parents report similar struggles at home. Which of the following disorders could Kelly's symptoms be consistent with?

a. Specific learning disability
b. Autism spectrum disorder
c. Generalized anxiety disorder
d. Attention-deficit hyperactivity disorder

88. Which of the following is a benefit of utilizing an electronic or online survey to collect student perception data following a counseling group?

a. An electronic or online survey best maintains student confidentiality.
b. An electronic or online survey allows for more questions to be asked.
c. An electronic or online survey allows for instant data collection.
d. An electronic or online survey is faster to create and administer.

89. A high school counselor would like to help rising ninth-grade students and their parents better understand the graduation requirements and course options in order to increase the school's four-year graduation rate. Which of the following is NOT a Behavior Standard from the ASCA Mindsets & Behaviors for Student Success that would be supported by this program?

a. Actively engaging in challenging coursework
b. Identifying long- and short- term academic, career, and social/emotional goals
c. Self-confidence in the ability to succeed
d. Creating relationships with adults that support success

90. Which of the following terms describes the consistency of an assessment?

a. Reliability
b. Validity
c. Standard deviation
d. Stanine

91. A student's standardized score report for academic assessment indicates that their stanine score is 8. Which of the following is a correct interpretation of this information?

a. The student's score is far below average.
b. The student's score is below average.
c. The student's score is average.
d. The student's score is above average.

Refer to the following for question 92:

Ms. White, a high school counselor, is planning a small group focused on improving study skills. As part of the group, she has students complete an electronic survey describing their independent use of various study skills in the first group meeting, and she plans to have them complete another survey in the last group meeting. After a few group sessions, she notices that one group member continually asks other students if they are doing their homework, using their study skills, and focusing in class. This student reminds their peers that they are supposed to be doing their assignments and studying regularly.

92. Which group role is this student demonstrating?

a. Scapegoat
b. Gatekeeper
c. Energizer
d. Interrogator

93. Which of the following data points is most likely to assist a school counselor in advocating for the assignment of appropriate duties within their school?

a. Use-of-time assessment analysis
b. School Counselor Performance Appraisal
c. Program goal analysis
d. School data profile analysis

94. A school intervention team is reviewing a functional behavior assessment to create a behavior intervention plan. When the team analyzes the data, which of the following would NOT be a possible function of the behavior?

a. Escape
b. Access
c. Sensory
d. Communication

95. Which of the following is an example of a technological resource that could be utilized in the Management component of the ASCA National Model?

a. An electronic calendar tracking a counselor's use of time throughout the school year
b. An electronic survey measuring student mastery of learning objectives from a classroom guidance lesson
c. A searchable bank of lesson plans aligned to the ASCA Mindsets & Behaviors for Student Success
d. An online college search database that connects career goals to available programs

96. In peer mediation programs, students are trained to guide peers through a conflict resolution process based on which of the following conflict resolution styles?

a. Competing
b. Collaborating
c. Avoiding
d. Accommodating

97. A counselor is working individually with a student toward their goal of developing friendships and feeling more connected at school. According to the theory of solution-focused brief therapy, how would the counselor approach termination of the student's individual counseling sessions?

a. Wait until the student reports that they are at a 10/10 on the scaling question.
b. Terminate after six sessions, as anything longer is not "brief."
c. Ask the student how they will know when they no longer need individual counseling.
d. Wait until the counselor observes that the student has achieved their goal.

98. Which of the following school counselor roles is considered a direct service?

a. Consulting
b. Collaborating
c. Evaluating
d. Counseling

99. In order to plan for the upcoming school year, a school counselor completes an annual agreement with their principal. Which of the following is NOT a component of the annual agreement?

a. Calendar of events and activities for the year
b. Counselor's responsibilities and use of time
c. Program goals aligned with the school's mission
d. Areas of professional development for the counselor

100. A school counselor who is leading a group counseling session wishes to stop a group member from monopolizing the conversation and allow others more floor time to participate. Which skill would the counselor utilize to accomplish this goal?

a. Summarizing
b. Blocking
c. Linking
d. Active listening

101. Which of the following is true about the role of a School Counselor Performance Appraisal in an ASCA National Model program?

a. The School Counselor Performance Appraisal is not part of an ASCA National Model program, but is a licensure requirement in many states.
b. The School Counselor Performance Appraisal is a self-evaluation completed by the school counselor once a year.
c. The School Counselor Performance Appraisal is conducted by an administrator once a year using school, district, or state guidelines.
d. The School Counselor Performance Appraisal is based on an administrator's observations of the school counselor.

102. Which of the following statements is NOT true regarding academic outcomes for students from low-SES backgrounds?

a. Students from low-SES backgrounds typically have less access to college information than their middle- or high-SES peers.
b. The high school graduation rate is lower among low-SES students than middle- or high-SES students.
c. Students from low-SES backgrounds typically have lower reading and language skills than their middle- or high-SES peers.
d. The academic achievement of students from low-SES backgrounds is more affected by their home and family conditions than their school conditions.

103. Mr. Scott is a new school counselor and is starting to collect data to plan his comprehensive school counseling program. Which of the following is a type of perception data that could be used to plan a new comprehensive school counseling program?

a. School data profile
b. Needs assessment
c. Pre-test data
d. Achievement testing data

104. A school counselor is working with a student who is struggling after receiving a B grade on a test. This student has historically gotten all As and tells the counselor that they will "never get into college and will never be successful" because of this grade. Which of the following cognitive distortions is this student expressing?

a. Personalization
b. Emotional reasoning
c. Catastrophizing
d. Labeling

105. Which of the following scenarios would be in alignment with the ASCA Ethical Standards for School Counselors?

a. A school counselor utilizes her social media account to post updates for students and parents about school events and college application deadlines.
b. A school counselor "follows" her students on social media so that she can keep tabs on their behavior and interactions with each other.
c. A school counselor who is having a hard time getting in touch with a student's parent sends the parent a private message on a social media platform.
d. A school counselor creates a separate social media account only for school-related updates that is linked to the official school social media account.

Refer to the following for question 106:

Mrs. Tucker, a high school counselor, is evaluating various drug and alcohol prevention curricula for use in her classroom guidance lessons. As a part of this, she is planning a parent information night about drug and alcohol prevention. She is beginning her session with information about risk and protective factors for student drug use.

106. Which of the following is NOT a protective factor that can reduce the likelihood of student drug use?

a. High self-esteem
b. Good grades
c. Strong peer groups
d. Supportive family relationships

107. Jasmine is an elementary school student who was recently diagnosed with ADHD. She struggles to complete tasks in the classroom and at home, sustain attention, and focus on assessments, and her impulsive behavior often results in her being sent to the office for discipline. Jasmine's psychologist recommended that Jasmine's parents ask for a Section 504 plan. Which of the following best describes the school counselor's role in Jasmine's Section 504 planning process?

a. The school counselor writes a plan of accommodations and modifications because Jasmine qualifies for a 504 plan with her ADHD diagnosis.
b. The school counselor conducts assessments and observations to determine Jasmine's current level of functioning at school and the need for accommodations and modifications.
c. The school counselor participates in a 504 team meeting to determine if Jasmine qualifies for a 504 plan and, if so, to advocate for appropriate accommodations and modifications.
d. The school counselor can work with Jasmine in individual counseling to address the social/emotional needs related to her ADHD diagnosis, however, participation in the 504 process is not appropriate for a school counselor.

108. Which of the following describes a classroom accommodation that is likely to be the most beneficial for a student who has difficulty seeing written content on the board?

a. Preferential seating
b. Extended time
c. Wearing glasses
d. Small group instruction

109. A school counselor learns during a parent conference regarding a child's attendance that the student's family was evicted from their apartment after the student's father lost his job. They have been living with a family member temporarily while the student's father continues to look for a new job. The family also faced the repossession of one of their vehicles, and the second vehicle is often used by the father while he applies for jobs. Which type of referral is most appropriate for the counselor to make in this situation?

a. The counselor does not need to make a referral because there is no abuse or neglect happening in this scenario and the student has adequate housing.
b. The counselor should refer the family to the county's housing services program to apply for a housing voucher.
c. The counselor should refer the family to the school's McKinney-Vento liaison for support, including transportation to school.
d. The counselor should refer the family to administration for an attendance plan because the child's transportation needs will continue to impact attendance.

110. Cognitive behavioral therapy relies on Albert Ellis's ABC model (originally developed as part of rational-emotive behavior therapy). What is the counselor analyzing when using the ABC model?

a. The client's environment
b. The client's emotional state
c. The client's thoughts or beliefs
d. The client's behaviors

111. Which of the following is NOT an assumption of developmental career theories?

a. The career development process includes various stages.
b. The process of choosing a career culminates in early adulthood.
c. Career choices are reversible and made throughout one's life.
d. Career development is an ongoing or longitudinal process.

112. Most approaches to career choice today are based on which theory?

a. Psychological
b. Trait-factor
c. Developmental
d. Social learning

113. According to Jean Piaget's theory of cognitive development, the majority of middle school students are in which stage of development?

a. The sensorimotor stage
b. The preoperational stage
c. The concrete operational stage
d. The formal operational stage

114. During a group counseling session, the group leader utilizes a role-playing intervention. Group members role-play interpersonal situations and the group provides feedback. This intervention is an example of the work conducted during which stage of the group counseling process?

a. Initial/forming
b. Transition/storming
c. Working/norming
d. Termination/adjourning

115. Which of the following topics or tasks would NOT be addressed in the group selection process for school-age children?

a. Informed consent
b. Voluntary participation
c. Parent permission
d. Allaying anxiety

116. Which combination best describes an ideal, closed-membership counseling group?

a. Homogeneous problem type and heterogeneous personality type
b. Homogeneous problem type and homogeneous personality type
c. Heterogeneous problem type and homogeneous personality type
d. Heterogeneous problem type and heterogeneous personality type

117. Which of the following is not a section within the Assess component of the ASCA National Model?

a. Program
b. School Counselor
c. Annual Results Reports
d. Student impact

118. Jim, a member of a counseling group focused on overcoming social anxiety, shares his recent success with utilizing skills learned from the group to navigate a tricky social situation. Jim is excited about his success and how the skills he learned helped him in that situation; the other members of the group are excited for him as well. Which benefit of group counseling would be directly demonstrated by this scenario?

a. Installation of hope
b. Universality
c. Group cohesiveness
d. Imparting information

119. Which of the following activities within an ASCA National Model program allows a school counselor to demonstrate a leadership role?

a. Define and share counseling program mission and vision statements.
b. Refer students to community agencies for mental health counseling.
c. Participate as part of an IEP team for a student with a learning disability.
d. Create an advisory council and discuss program outcomes.

120. Which of the following is an ASCA-recommended procedure following a natural disaster?

a. Ensure students have access to multiple news outlets for updated information.
b. Modify/shorten the daily schedule to reduce stress on students.
c. Limit student discussion of the disaster to reduce the focus on the disaster.
d. Be honest with students and share as much developmentally appropriate information as possible.

Answer Key and Explanations for Test #2

1. D: The system support component of the comprehensive school counseling program utilizes a counselor's leadership skills to support the total school environment and promote systemic change. System support activities such as professional development, committee work, and program management all provide opportunities for school counselors to demonstrate leadership and advocacy at the school level. While there could be some components of counseling curriculum, individual student planning, and responsive services that allow a counselor to demonstrate leadership, the system support or indirect services component is more strongly related to leadership roles.

2. A: The define component contains these standards. The define component of the ASCA National Model seeks to define school counseling as a profession and sets the parameters for quality school counseling programs. The manage component of the model aims to provide school counselors with the frameworks and tools they need to make their school counseling program successful. The deliver component of the model helps school counselors provide appropriate services to their students, directly or indirectly, in order to improve student achievement and behavior. The assess component of the model encourages school counselors to regularly assess their school counseling activities to ensure they are effective.

3. A: Scaling questions are a key component of solution-focused brief counseling and are used to help the client notice improvements toward their goal. Other examples of solution-focused brief counseling techniques include asking about exceptions, the miracle question, and assigning homework suggestions. Free association is a technique more typically utilized by a classical psychoanalyst (such as Sigmund Freud). Changing self-talk is commonly associated with rational-emotive behavior therapy (Albert Ellis), which assumes that the root of the client's emotional disturbance lies in their irrational thoughts, and therefore changing cognitions can change the client's emotional state. The empty chair technique is a Gestalt technique (Fritz Perls) where the client directs conversation about their thoughts and feelings toward an empty chair as if the person they are speaking to is sitting in it.

4. B: IDEA (the Individuals with Disabilities Education Act) guarantees children with disabilities the right to a free and appropriate public education. There are multiple components that an IEP team may include in a child's particular plan to best support their specific needs. At its core, an IEP requires specialized instruction to meet the child's needs. Additional components of the IEP can include accommodations and modifications, such as extended time on tests or written copies of class notes and related services such as speech therapy or occupational therapy, all provided free of charge to the student. In addition, IDEA requires that children with disabilities are educated in the least restrictive environment (LRE) necessary to meet that child's specific needs. A common example of an LRE would be the regular education classroom. What IDEA does not require is preferential treatment or guaranteed participation in athletics or extracurriculars. While students need to be provided an equal access opportunity, they are not guaranteed a participating position in these activities.

5. D: Social bullying is bullying that focuses on damaging or reducing a victim's social relationships, including exclusion or spreading rumors. Social bullying is most common in female students. While middle school boys are more likely to experience or participate in physical bullying, such as hitting, kicking, or fighting, they are not immune to social bullying. Cyberbullying can be a form of social or verbal bullying, including name-calling, spreading rumors, making threats, exclusion, and other types of harassment; cyberbullying is common at the middle school level. Finally, many bullying prevention programs identify various roles students play in bullying, including the role of "bystander" or "onlooker," a student who witnesses bullying but does nothing to stop the bully or support the victim; a student in this role is considered to be supporting the bullying behavior.

6. C: According to the ASCA National Model, it is not appropriate for school counselors to be a part of issuing student discipline or be responsible for clerical tasks such as schedule changes. School counselors are an appropriate member of a team responsible for planning a comprehensive, schoolwide anti-bullying program.

7. A: Development of the mission and vision statements for the counseling program establishes the program focus and defines student outcomes, which are part of the Define component of the ASCA National Model. Implementation of the vision and mission statements usually falls under the Manage component.

8. D: Performing disciplinary actions or assigning disciplinary consequences is never an appropriate duty for school counselors. School counselors may support administrators by counseling students who have disciplinary problems, helping to identify and resolve student issues, advocating for students, or analyzing discipline data. Effective school counselors can be important members of the school-based team, but it is not appropriate for school counselors to take on administrative roles.

9. D: Carl Rogers' person-centered therapy, also known as client-centered therapy or nondirective counseling, focuses on three key factors: congruence, also known as genuineness or authenticity; unconditional positive regard, the concept of the therapist accepting the client no matter what they do; and empathy, or the therapist's ability to feel what the client is feeling. According to Rogers, if these three required conditions are met in an effective helping relationship, the client can develop positively. Transference describes the scenario in which a client projects their feelings or emotions onto the therapist.

10. A: The Strong Interest Inventory is a career assessment that helps align an individual's interests to different career types. The six categories of interests (Realistic, Artistic, Investigative, Social, Enterprising, and Conventional) can help an individual learn about careers that others with similar interests enjoy or are well suited for. Like nearly all assessments, the Strong Interest Inventory should not be used as a sole data point for decision making. It would be inappropriate for a counselor to encourage or discourage a student from taking certain types of courses based solely on the results of this assessment. It should be used as a tool to help students learn more about themselves and the careers available to them, but it is not the only tool for those purposes.

11. D: A well-designed needs assessment can be a powerful tool for school counselors in identifying areas of need, defining goals, and planning programming. Needs assessments can also identify areas where there may be equity gaps, individual student concerns, or common student concerns that may be addressed by small-group counseling. While it may be tempting to use a needs assessment to track changes in data from year to year as a form of program evaluation, this is not the purpose for which they are designed, and they are unlikely to be effective for program evaluation due to changes in student enrollment or staffing from year to year and a lack of specificity within the questions to evaluate individual programs.

12. C: In this example, the school counselor is seeking information from the speech therapist, the expert in stuttering. This is an example of consultation performed to benefit a student. Each of the other examples listed is an example of collaboration.

13. C: Outcome data provides a means to measure the effectiveness of a program or activity. In this case, the outcome data is focused on student achievement. The data is focused on the entire school population and is not disaggregated by subgroups, so choice D does not apply. Activity evaluation data focuses on participants' perceptions or opinions after an intervention or activity and is a type of perception data. If the school counselor had surveyed graduates to gather their opinions of the school's program to improve graduation rates, that would have been activity evaluation data. Competency attainment data measures student mastery of a specific competency or objective. An example related to graduation rates would be the percentage of students in a given grade level who have a completed four-year graduation plan on file.

14. C: Making a gentle connection between group members is an appropriate strategy to draw out a quiet group member; this skill is known as "linking." Ignoring the fact that James is not participating in the group is not appropriate, as other group members may begin to focus on James's non-participation by trying to draw him out or by becoming withdrawn themselves. Pulling an individual group member aside during a group session is typically not appropriate, as it takes the focus away from the group's collective focus, and removing a member from the group can shake the trust of the remaining group members.

15. C: Calculating grade point averages is an inappropriate activity for school counselors, according to the ASCA National Model. Providing core classroom guidance curriculum is an appropriate direct service, as is counseling students about appropriate dress for school. While counselors should not be responsible for maintaining student records, it is appropriate for counselors to ensure regulations are followed in the maintenance of those records.

16. D: When it comes to kindergarten readiness, school counselors have the opportunity to participate in planning for comprehensive transitional support. Starting kindergarten is considered one of the biggest transitions of a young child's life, and many students struggle to adapt; school counselors have the skills and abilities to support teachers, students, and parents through this transition. Remember that administering assessments or processing paperwork such as enrollments falls outside of the appropriate roles for school counselors outlined by ASCA. Many school districts require students whose parents wish for them to enter kindergarten before they turn 5 years old to complete a comprehensive "early kindergarten entry assessment." Typically, these are conducted by a psychologist; such assessments would not be appropriate for the school counselor to conduct.

17. C: With programs aimed at increasing graduation rates, outcome data such as the four-year graduation rate is often the primary piece of data that is highlighted; an effective counselor examines graduation rates even further by disaggregating data into student subgroups in order to identify gaps in achievement. Changes in this rate over time are also important in identifying areas of need or improvements made as a result of school counseling programs. School counselors also impact student mindsets and behaviors through their interventions, and perception data is an important method of measuring how students feel, what they think they know, and what they believe. Answer choice C represents a piece of perception data gathered through a student survey, possibly in a pre- and post-test format, that provides the counselor with information about the effectiveness of their intervention on their students' beliefs. Answer choices A and B represent process data, which is another important type of data to evaluate when evaluating program effectiveness.

18. C: ASCA does not support school counselors in taking on the role of schoolwide testing coordinator because this task detracts from the role of a counselor in providing academic, social/emotional, and career support to students.

19. B: The Strong Interest Inventory is a career assessment designed to help individuals understand their interests and how they relate to different types of careers. The Strong Interest Inventory is based on the work of John Holland and the concept that people with similar interests work in similar careers.

20. C: School counselors support the implementation of MTSS by providing a standards-based curriculum to all students (the intervener role). It is not appropriate for school counselors to lead the implementation of MTSS as a whole because MTSS is a team approach. Even within an MTSS framework, it is still inappropriate for a school counselor to coordinate a testing program or to provide standard individual counseling to all students in a certain tier of MTSS.

21. D: Consultation is an important role for school counselors in supporting student achievement, advocating for students, and understanding student needs. Because consultation is not directly working with the student, it is considered an indirect service. Responsive services (such as counseling and crisis response), individual student planning (appraisal and advisement), and school counseling core curriculum (small group counseling, classroom guidance) are all direct student services.

22. C: The ASCA Ethical Standards for School Counselors and the ACA Code of Ethics both address confidentiality and should serve as a reference for ethical decision making for school counselors facing ethical dilemmas. In addition, school counselors should consult state laws to determine the appropriate course of action for their contexts before acting. States vary slightly in reporting and confidentiality requirements and occasionally change. There are instances when there are ethically sound reasons for breaching confidentiality, however, the ethical standards describe these circumstances as those in which the student is facing "serious foreseeable harm."

23. C: Closing-the-gap action plan documents are used to develop plans to address discrepancies between groups of students. In the situation described, there appears to be a discrepancy between students with disabilities and nondisabled students in the rate of high school graduation, so a closing-the-gap action plan would be appropriate. Within that plan, a counselor may identify activities for classroom guidance lessons or small group counseling, but the overall plan to address the discrepancy is the closing-the-gap action plan. In addition, the documentation of activities and evaluation methods takes place within the closing-the-gap action plan template.

24. D: This situation most likely calls for an intermediate intervention. Broad, proactive measures such as a parent information night or classroom guidance likely would not address the needs of this specific group of students who are already failing classes. In many schools, this would be considered a tier II intervention, which is a more targeted intervention for students who are exhibiting academic difficulties. A special education referral would not be appropriate at this level, as other intermediate interventions have not yet been put into place.

25. B: Any form of electronic communication between the school counselor and other school officials can create an official school record that needs to be treated appropriately under FERPA, even if student names are not used. All forms of electronic communication should adhere to the ethical standards, and special care should be taken to protect confidentiality by utilizing accepted security standards. The ASCA Ethical Standards encourage counselors to take care in purging electronic sole-possession case notes, similar to hard-copy sole possession case notes.

26. D: While immigration is a thorny issue, the Supreme Court ruling *Plyler v. Doe* (1982) is clear in stating that no student, regardless of immigration status, can be prohibited from accessing public K-12 education. Further, the official ASCA Position Statement on this topic states that school counselors have an ethical duty to advocate for equal access to curriculum and services for all students, regardless of immigration status. A comprehensive school counseling program provides academic, social/emotional, and career components for all students.

27. C: Cultural bias is a potentially significant problem affecting the validity of tests and should be considered not only when selecting and administering tests but also when interpreting test results. Cultural bias occurs when differences in test-takers' gender, race, ethnicity, or socioeconomic status impact their background knowledge, understanding of test items, or understanding of the behaviors required to successfully complete a test. For example, a test that includes an English idiom in a math question may not be accessible for English language learners, and their success on that test item could be affected due to their English proficiency, rather than their math ability. A test item asking students to complete a phrase from a nursery rhyme may not be accessible to students from a culture that does not practice or sing that nursery rhyme, or a reading passage that references polo may be confusing for students who do not have background knowledge related to polo due to their socioeconomic status or culture. Differences in classroom groupings would not result in a cultural bias, but they could result in a difference in instructional quality or curriculum taught, which could affect student outcomes on tests.

28. A: Generally speaking, classroom guidance is a preventative activity; it is systematically delivered to all students. Intervention activities take place when an issue or problem is identified, therefore an activity that is systematically delivered to all students is not an intervention activity. Outreach involves "reaching out" of the school and into the community, and classroom guidance does not fit this description. While classroom guidance may be focused on academic topics, "academic" is not a type of counseling activity.

29. B: For a test to be standardized, the test questions, instructions, and testing procedures need to be consistent. Educators who administer standardized tests such as the SAT or end-of-grade tests are likely familiar with the requirements to read instructions from a script, carefully time the test administration, and maintain the consistency of the test format among test-takers. The age of the test-takers, however, has no impact on the standardization of the test itself. For example, many younger students take the SAT as part of gifted education programs or for practice for the future. If standardized test results are norm-referenced, the ages of test-takers could affect the norming group, but they do not affect the standardization of the test itself.

30. D: While these types of requests are common, they can still represent an ethical dilemma for school counselors. A child's educational record is protected under FERPA, so this information cannot be shared with an outside agency without parental consent. Oftentimes, the information being requested is helpful for the clinician in developing and monitoring a child's treatment goals. Sometimes, a request from an agency will already have a parent signature on it, in which case it is best to consult your school policy on how to proceed. Many schools still require the counselor to obtain parental consent on their own version of a consent form before communicating with an outside agency in any way, whether that is a phone call or a copy of a record.

31. C: Special education evaluations should be comprehensive evaluations that utilize a variety of data from multiple sources. End-of-grade standardized test scores should never be the sole data point to qualify or disqualify a child from receiving special education services.

32. B: There are three types of action plans that can be created as part of a comprehensive school counseling program: curriculum action plan, small-group action plan, and closing-the-gap action plan. Therefore, the three corresponding results reports to analyze the effectiveness of these action plans are the curriculum results report, small-group results report, and closing-the-gap results report. There is not an individual counseling action plan or results report.

33. C: School counselors should never be the sole decision-makers in any part of the IEP process; instead, they should serve as members of a multi-disciplinary team working together to meet the needs of students with special needs. According to ASCA, school counselors provide only short-term, goal-focused counseling as an IEP-related service; long-term or therapeutic counseling should be provided by other qualified mental health professionals (e.g., school psychologists, social workers, or community providers) rather than being written into an IEP as a school counselor service. Writing and determining the specific social-emotional goals in the IEP is the responsibility of the entire IEP team and typically the special education case manager; the school counselor contributes data and suggestions but does not unilaterally write IEP goals. Therefore, (C) is not an accurate description of the counselor's role, whereas (A), (B), and (D) are.

34. C: Student work samples are a useful data source for a wide variety of purposes. Student English proficiency, mastery of academic standards, progress toward academic goals, the impact of academic interventions, and the effectiveness of instructional strategies are examples of evaluations that can be conducted with student work samples as a data source. An autism evaluation, however, does not utilize student work samples because it is not an academically based diagnosis.

35. A: Conducting a program evaluation is an important component of a comprehensive school counseling program, and sharing the results is part of the evaluation process. According to ASCA, the goals of sharing these results are to "promote understanding, increase the value of and promote respect and indispensability for the work of professional school counselors." ASCA recommends sharing with a variety of stakeholders, including faculty, administrators, and community members. Therefore, those methods that effectively communicate counseling program results to a wide variety of stakeholders in a clear, easy-to-access, and easy-to-understand format are the most desirable methods.

36. C: Observations are a frequently used method of gathering behavioral data for behavior intervention plans or assessing the instructional environment. They would not be an appropriate method of evaluating a child for a disability or special education services without being combined with other assessments. Assessing instructional interventions also requires additional assessments or data points, such as formative assessment data.

37. D: Process data is information that describes when, how, and with whom an intervention or program took place. The number of participants, the number of sessions, and the timing or duration of a program are all examples of information that is conveyed through process data. Student feedback or pre- and post-tests are types of perception data, while student grade point averages are an example of outcome data.

38. A: Consulting involves a counselor gathering or sharing information about a student or group of students. In consultation, school counselors may share strategies that support student achievement with various stakeholders, advocate for students, or receive information from others to identify student needs and appropriate strategies to support them. Generally, consultation features one person presenting information to others or seeking information from others. Collaboration is different in that school counselors work together with others to think of solutions or strategies for student success, and all parties are working together toward a common goal. Evaluation is the process by which a school counselor collects and analyzes data about their comprehensive school counseling program to determine strengths and areas of improvement. Counseling is a direct service to students, such as individual or small group counseling.

39. B: Cognitive behavioral therapy focuses on changing thought patterns that contribute to undesired outcomes. In this case, the counselor wants to alter Annie's anxiety about school performance. While each of the other answer options may be a consideration depending on the scenario, none of them represent a cognitive behavioral approach.

40. C: According to the ASCA Ethical Standards for School Counselors, counselors should evaluate any personal biases that may prevent them from providing comprehensive services to all students. When school counselors identify biases that interfere with providing comprehensive services to all students, they should seek additional training and development rather than deny counseling services to these students based on their personal biases. School counselors should work to promote an environment that respects diversity.

41. B: Title II of the Education Amendments of 1976, which updated the 1963 Vocational Education Act, focused on reducing biases in vocational education as well as increasing equity and access to vocational education. The overall goal of Title II was to make vocational education more equitable on the basis of gender. Answer A is more closely aligned with Title IX, which focuses on sex discrimination in educational access and is often referenced in sexual harassment cases. Answer C focuses on Section 504, which protects disabled students from discrimination. Answer D references FERPA.

42. A: Achievement tests measure how well the test-taker has mastered specific skills or objectives. End-of-grade or end-of-course tests, as required by many states and school districts, are examples of achievement tests because they measure a student's mastery of the content objectives or skills that are generally expected to be taught during that grade level or course. While some schools may use data from these achievement tests to make placement decisions for future courses, that is not what these types of tests are designed for. Aptitude tests are a different type of assessment that attempts to predict the test-taker's aptitude or future success in a specific area, while placement tests measure the test-taker's skill level in a specific content area in order to determine their current level for course placements. Norm-referenced tests measure the individual test-taker's or group of test-takers' results against another group of test-takers, while criterion-referenced tests measure the individual test-taker's results against a specific set of standards. For example, a norm-referenced test may indicate that a student's mathematics ability is more or less advanced than a group of their same-aged peers, while a criterion-referenced test would simply indicate that a student has mastered all of their current grade-level mathematics standards.

43. C: Perception data is data that measures what participants think they know, believe, or can do. This type of data is typically measured in the form of feedback surveys or pre- and post-tests. This is not the only type of data that can be analyzed to determine the effectiveness of a classroom guidance curriculum and identify areas for improvement. Answer choices A and D represent process data, and answer choice B represents outcome data. A thorough evaluation of the classroom guidance curriculum would include each of these types of data to identify both the effectiveness of the program and any potential areas of improvement.

44. A: A reinforcement is a consequence that increases the likelihood of the target behavior happening again. Reinforcements can be positive or negative. Positive reinforcements reward the target behavior with something pleasant or enjoyable, while negative reinforcements reward the target behavior with the removal of something unpleasant or undesirable. B.F. Skinner's famous experiment involved rats who pushed a lever to escape a painful electric current, which was a negative reinforcement. Punishment is the opposite of reinforcement, as it decreases the likelihood of the behavior happening again. Neutral consequences do not affect the frequency of the target behavior.

45. C: Title IX, often known as a sports law, requires schools to have equal athletic opportunities for male and female students. However, sex discrimination also applies to a variety of other forms of discrimination, including sexual harassment. In this case, the boys at school are creating a hostile environment, and the case should be pursued as a sexual harassment case. Each school and/or district has specific Title IX policies that school counselors should familiarize themselves with. Title IX requires schools to take prompt and effective action to correct a hostile environment, even if the student does not follow the published grievance procedure.

46. C: Assisting students with course selections to help students make choices that are rigorous and align with their post-secondary plans is an appropriate activity for a school counselor. Understanding appropriate and inappropriate counseling tasks is a major focus of the Management section of the ASCA National Model; this is an area that school counselors should be very familiar with in order to plan their use of time and advocate for appropriate duties. A comprehensive school counseling program designed with the ASCA National Model will focus on prevention, intervention, and advocacy, not clerical or administrative tasks. When it comes to assisting students with post-secondary plans, there are many tasks that school counselors may have done historically or may still do in some schools that are not considered appropriate activities. These include tasks such as calculating class rank or grade point average, coordinating schoolwide SAT testing, copying student records for college applications, or doing other clerical tasks related to college applications.

47. A: Many of the communication and active listening techniques employed by peer mediation programs to resolve student conflicts are the same types of techniques and skills used by counselors in individual counseling. "I think you should..." is a phrase that implies giving advice, which is not productive in a peer mediation process (or in individual counseling). Peer mediation programs focus on training students to facilitate collaboration between peers, not resolve their conflicts for them. "Can you tell me more?" is a probing question, "What I hear you saying is..." is a paraphrase, and "I can see why you feel that way" is a validating statement; all of these are appropriate and helpful techniques in peer mediation.

48. D: The use-of-time assessment is an ASCA National Model document, but it is not an action plan. The use-of-time assessment analyzes the counselor's activities over the course of the school year and is typically done twice per year; as an assessment, it is a look backward over activities already conducted rather than a data-driven plan for future actions. Curriculum action plans, small-group action plans, and closing-the-gap action plans are all data-driven planning documents that help the counselor design interventions for the future. The curriculum action plan helps counselors create an effective plan for implementing the school counseling curriculum, and the small-group action plan is a similar document for planning small-group interventions. Closing-the-gap action plans help counselors design interventions focused on addressing discrepancies in academic or behavioral outcome data between student groups.

49. B: According to ASCA, clerical tasks, including maintaining student records, are inappropriate activities for school counselors. Appropriate tasks include interpretation of records and data.

50. C: A school counselor should maintain confidentiality for their students, so seeking out information about community resources or mental health services utilized by students could pose a confidentiality issue. If agencies are utilized by other students that the counselor is aware of, the counselor should be careful to protect the privacy and confidentiality of those students in providing referral lists. To protect the counselor from liability, any referral lists should be vetted and approved by the school or district in accordance with district policy. It is always a good idea to contact individual agencies to find out if they are open and accepting new referrals, and to gather information about services provided and how to make a referral because the availability of these services can change very quickly.

51. D: The ASCA Ethical Standards for School Counselors indicate that counselors have a duty to refer when students need a higher level of support than a counselor can adequately provide. In making referrals, counselors should be careful not to endorse any specific provider and, when possible, should provide parents with a vetted list of possible counselors that is approved by the district. The duty to refer does not apply to counselors who feel that they cannot provide services to a student based on their personal or religious beliefs; in those scenarios, counselors should seek additional training and development.

52. C: A summative assessment is designed to be given at the conclusion of a unit of study, course, or grade level to measure learning outcomes and mastery of content standards. A summative assessment compares an individual's performance to the standards expected to be taught during the period being tested. A formative assessment is an assessment that is given during the unit of study, course, or grade level to monitor student learning and provide feedback to the instructor in order to adjust, reteach, or modify instruction going forward. A diagnostic assessment is typically given at the start of a unit of study, course, or grade level to determine the individual's prior knowledge or current level of performance in order to guide instruction, identify areas of need, or provide a benchmark for measuring growth when compared to a summative assessment. A norm-referenced assessment compares an individual's performance to a group of peers rather than to a set of standards or objectives to be mastered.

53. A: The Wechsler Intelligence Scale for Children (WISC) is a commonly used tool in a psycho-educational evaluation, typically as part of a special education evaluation; however, it is inappropriate to use an intelligence test as the sole basis for special education placement decisions. For example, if a student has a suspected learning disability, an average or above-average IQ score should not be used to deny them special education services. It is also inappropriate to use IQ test results to choose students' coursework, career guidance, or college options. Assessments represent only one data point in making decisions about a student's education.

54. B: The ASCA Mindsets & Behaviors for Student Success are the most current version of student standards outlined by ASCA. They update and replace the previous ASCA National Standards for Students. Each of the 36 standards outlined in the Mindsets & Behaviors can be applied to each of the three domains (academic, social/emotional, career). The Mindsets & Behaviors are not broken down into specific grade-level competencies but can be aligned to Common Core or other state standards that are delineated by grade-level competencies.

55. B: Students with disabilities frequently require accommodations or modifications during standardized testing in order to allow the student to demonstrate their knowledge effectively and reduce the impact of their disability on the assessment results. With standardized tests, however, it is also important for the test administration to be as consistent as possible among students so that the test results are reliable and valid. The student specifically is struggling with reading assessments, so having the test read aloud would not be an appropriate modification because that affects the validity of the test (reading the test aloud makes it a listening test, not a reading test). Each of the other accommodations listed would generally be appropriate as a testing accommodation for students with attention difficulties.

56. A: The school counselor has a duty to breach confidentiality and warn parents or guardians if there is a risk of serious and foreseeable harm to a student. While Janice claims that her comments were not serious, ethically the counselor alone should not make a determination of risk and is obligated to warn Janice's parents of her threat.

57. A: In situations where a student's mental health needs are beyond the scope of the school counselor's expertise and training, an outside referral is the most appropriate step. In addition, students with concerns that would require long-term individual counseling should be referred for outside counseling, as long-term counseling is beyond the training and ability of a school counselor with a large caseload. School counselors should follow school and district policies in providing parents and families with agencies for referrals, and typically referrals will include a list of agencies to choose from. While seeking additional training and professional development is likely to benefit both the counselor and the student, this scenario makes it clear that Joey needs professional mental health support. Small group counseling can be beneficial for many students, but Joey clearly needs more than that.

58. B: Psychological career theory, also known as personality career theory, focuses on an individual's personality type and the types of careers that best fit that personality type. A psychological or personality approach will always begin with a self-directed search to determine the individual's personality type. Researching careers that students are already interested in, or learning about the skills and abilities needed in those careers, are common activities in many schools, but these do not fit the psychological career theory whereby individuals are matched to potential careers based on their personality type. Before researching careers, students would need to take the personality survey to determine which types of careers are best suited for their personality type. A field trip to visit a real-life work setting would be more aligned with a social learning career theory, such as the approach developed by John Krumboltz. A social learning career theory is based on the concept that interests are learned, so exposure to a variety of careers and work sites gives an individual more learning and experiences from which to develop their interests.

59. B: ASCA has a large body of research, including topics such as counseling theory and techniques, effectiveness of counseling programs, and the ASCA National Model. Counselors can utilize the thorough research published by ASCA to support their advocacy efforts, including the recommended student-to-counselor ratio of 250:1. School counselors can support their request at their own school or district level using their individual program data (such as the use-of-time assessment, annual calendar, or Recognized ASCA Model Program application) but are likely to find that nationwide, peer-reviewed data is more effectively leveraged in their efforts.

60. C: In this situation, the counselor needs more information before determining next steps. Talking to Sally privately will help the counselor determine what is happening and how to proceed.

61. C: The working or "norming" stage of the group counseling process is where the majority of the group's time is spent, usually about 50% of the time. This is where the majority of the group goals are addressed and the true "work" of group counseling is accomplished. The initial or "forming" stage is when the group first comes together, goals and group rules are established, and the facilitator tries to alleviate members' anxiety about the group counseling process. The transition or "storming" stage is when the group begins to transition to the actual work of the group counseling process. This stage is characterized by conflict and group members challenging the facilitator. If conflicts are not resolved in this stage, the result can be difficult for the remainder of the group counseling session. Finally, termination or "adjourning" is the closing of the group, sometimes characterized by the grief of group members, and is focused on transferring new skills or experiences to the outside world.

62. B: Alfred Adler's theory of individual psychology focused on feelings of inferiority vs. superiority, and Adlerian therapy investigates the effect of the client's birth order on behavior. Adler was once a colleague of Sigmund Freud, but he eventually separated from Freud's circles.

63. C: A simple checklist to record the number of times the target behavior occurs, as well as a way to record the circumstances surrounding the behavior (such as time of day, type of instruction, or level of structure), would be useful to help the intervention team. This would help to notice trends or patterns and identify environmental or procedural modifications that could support appropriate behavior. A simple tally sheet, however, would not provide enough detail about the behavior to develop an intervention. A tally sheet may be appropriate to document improvements in the target behavior once an intervention is in place. In this situation, a functional behavior assessment is premature. Functional behavior assessments are appropriate for high-intensity behaviors or those behaviors that have not responded to lower-level interventions. While observations can be useful in many situations, they are typically utilized to supplement other types of data rather than used as stand-alone data.

64. D: A tier II intervention is typically a small, group-level intervention for those students who have demonstrated a need for a higher level of support. These are intermediate-level interventions between tier I (whole-class or whole-school instructional practices) and tier III (individualized, intensive interventions). Therefore, small group instruction is the only choice that represents an intermediate, small group level intervention.

65. C: The Deliver component of the comprehensive school counseling program includes all types of direct and indirect services, which ideally make up 80% or more of a counselor's time. The Deliver component includes instruction, appraisal and advisement, and counseling; these services are delivered through individual counseling, small groups, and classroom lessons.

66. A: The school data profile is an important tool provided within the ASCA National Model to assist counselors in disaggregating student data. This data can be collected both short- and long-term and in a variety of areas, including achievement and behavioral data. The school data profile can be used to both manage the school counseling program (by identifying areas of focus for closing-the-gap action plans or advocating for equity issues) and evaluate the school counseling program (by analyzing long-term data to understand the impact of the program). Attainment of competencies and needs assessment data are types of perception data that can be difficult to represent in a spreadsheet, especially if the data is more qualitative in nature. Attainment of competencies data is process data that could be prepared in a spreadsheet but is not the focus of the school data profile.

67. B: Frank Parsons developed the trait-factor approach to career counseling. The trait-factor approach utilizes data from tests to match an individual with one best career. Therefore, a strictly trait-factor approach would begin with testing to determine Grace's traits. Trait-factor approaches do not rely on objective data from conversations. The Self-Directed Search from answer choice D refers to a tool used in John Holland's personality theory of career counseling.

68. A: According to the ASCA Ethical Standards for School Counselors, a counselor's primary obligation is to protect the student's right to confidentiality. The Ethical Standards indicate that the counselor should balance this right with an understanding of the rights of parents to be "the guiding voice in their children's lives." Particularly when there is a risk of serious and foreseeable harm to the student, a student's right to confidentiality may need to be breached to prevent such harm and protect the rights of the parents.

69. B: A percentile rank is a method of comparing an individual test-taker to a group of their peers. In other words, for standardized test scores, a percentile rank could describe a student's achievement in comparison with their same-age peers. A percentile rank is not the same as a percentage, which would be a way of describing the number of test items answered correctly. A percentile rank does not give any information about what a test-taker does or does not know, but rather how their knowledge or achievement compares to a norm-referenced group (typically for standardized tests, the norm-referenced group is the student's same-age or same-grade peers). If a student's standardized test score is in the 50th percentile on a standardized test, that means their score is the same as or better than 50 percent of their peers. A percentile rank between the 23rd and 76th percentile is considered "average."

70. B: In this scenario, the counselor is focused on establishing group cohesion, or relationships among group members. Group cohesion is an essential trait for a successful counseling group, as group members begin to focus on the work of solving their collective problems.

71. A: IDEA, the Individuals with Disabilities Education Act, provides for the education of children with disabilities by requiring schools to provide a free appropriate public education through an individualized education plan (IEP) to children with disabilities in one of thirteen categories. These categories are: autism, deaf-blindness, developmental delay, emotional disturbance, hearing impairments (including deafness), intellectual disability, multiple disabilities, orthopedic impairments, other health impairments, specific learning disabilities, speech or language impairments, traumatic brain injury, and visual impairments (including blindness). Therefore, the school counselor would refer to the provisions of this law as well as school policies under IDEA to provide information to Hanna's parents. The other laws named in answer choices are Section 504, the Family Educational Rights and Privacy Act (FERPA), and the Every Student Succeeds Act (ESSA). Section 504 is also a disability-related law, but Section 504 addresses how a school will provide accommodations and modifications to remove the barriers a child's disability may create for accessing the curriculum; an IEP outlines a specific educational plan including specialized instruction. FERPA has to do with the privacy of student records, and ESSA is a federal law guiding K-12 public education policy.

72. A: The recommended and most commonly used practice for academic intervention plans is a strengths-based focus. Most students needing an academic intervention plan are already aware (or their parents and teachers are aware) of the problems they are facing. The school counselor's role in the academic intervention process is to identify the strengths the student has that may be supported in order to increase academic outcomes. The interventions designed in this type of plan are typically focused on either utilizing existing strengths or overcoming barriers. Cognitive behavioral therapy describes a method of one-on-one counseling, which at times may be a part of the plan, but it would not be the approach used to actually develop the plan. Family factors are often considered in developing academic intervention plans, but family therapy is not part of a school counselor's duties and should not be used to develop an academic intervention plan.

73. B: This scenario describes a collaborative effort between a parent and school counselor to help a student who is struggling. Collaboration is not just an activity between school staff, and it often includes parents or even students in the process. This could specifically be described as solution-focused collaboration, as the pair discussed previous successes and things that are going well. This is a frequently used and appropriate strategy for collaborating with parents.

74. C: In the industry vs. inferiority stage of development, an individual begins to compare their personal accomplishments (academic, relational, athletic, etc.) to their peers. As a result, they develop either a sense of pride or a sense of inferiority in comparison to others. The autonomy vs.

shame stage focuses on developing the senses of independence and autonomy in a child who is given the opportunity to make basic decisions about their life, or a sense of shame when the child is not given such opportunity. In the initiative vs. guilt stage, a child learns a sense of pride when allowed to work toward a goal and practice responsibility, or a sense of guilt when they are unsuccessful in this task. Identity vs. role confusion is the stage in which adolescents grapple with the question "Who am I?"

75. A: Thorough data analysis, including disaggregating data by subgroup, is typically used for either creating a closing-the-gap action plan or completing a school data profile. This type of data analysis is helpful for identifying potential achievement gaps or equity issues within the school or district that the counselor can plan to address with a closing-the-gap action plan. This type of detailed, schoolwide data analysis is typically not used for creating a small-group action plan, although a small group may be utilized as a strategy within a closing-the-gap action plan. The annual agreement is a document created between a counselor and an administrator to plan for and establish goals for the upcoming school year and is focused on the counseling program itself; a needs assessment is usually in the form of a survey completed by students, staff, and/or parents to identify strengths and areas of concern in the school.

76. B: This example describes collaboration and could also be considered an example of "leaderless" collaboration, where all parties in the collaborative effort have equal leadership status. Co-counselors within the same school may also conduct each of the other roles listed independently or together. For example, counselors may frequently consult with one another on particularly difficult cases, ethical dilemmas, or areas of individual expertise. Effective counselors will also likely conduct an evaluation of their programming together. Although likely less common in a school setting due to availability of time, counselors may also at times conduct counseling together, particularly in groups.

77. B: Online college searches provide a wide knowledge base that could not be achieved with the counselor's knowledge alone. A counselor should utilize all college search tools appropriately to help students learn more about various colleges, not to encourage or discourage students from applying to specific colleges. School counselors provide students with the information and tools to make informed choices about college applications and admissions, but they should not impose their beliefs about specific colleges or plans on students. An online search tool cannot replace the goal setting and individual planning achieved in face-to-face planning with a school counselor.

78. D: People often confuse "collaborative" and "compromising" solutions as the same type of solution, but they are different. Collaborative solutions are usually considered the ideal outcome of conflict resolution processes. In a collaborative solution, each party has their needs met and is satisfied with the outcome; this is also thought of as a "win-win" solution. Answer choice C would be a compromise solution, where each party gives up something they want in order to appease the other. A compromise may keep the peace on the surface, but oftentimes one or both parties are at least partially unsatisfied with the outcome. Both answer choices A and B describe accommodating styles, where one party acquiesces to the needs of the other.

79. C: Schools have various subtleties and names for the process of designing interventions for students, however, almost all schools have some type of formal intervention process. This may be called a multitiered system of supports (MTSS), response to intervention (RTI), student support team (SST), or a number of other names. Ultimately, the fundamental process is the same: Identify areas of concern and develop interventions to address those areas, then reassess after a specified amount of time to determine if progress is being made. While interventions such as individual counseling may be appropriate, the counselor and teacher would first need to identify specific areas of concern and determine if that intervention would be appropriate for Anthony. Typically, referrals for special education evaluations could occur as part of this intervention process, but they are almost never the first step to be taken.

80. B: Each of the symptoms described could be indicative of a vision problem. Before moving to a full educational evaluation for learning disabilities or other learning problems, a simple vision screening could help the student described overcome a barrier to learning. In many districts, a vision screening is a required step in the intervention process prior to any special education or psychological referrals. The behaviors described do not necessarily point to abuse or neglect, although the school social worker can be a resource in procuring free or low-cost medical eye exams and eyeglasses for students who do not pass their vision screening.

81. D: The ASCA Mindsets and Behaviors for Student Success represent the attitudes and behaviors essential for student success and can be applied to the academic, career, and social/emotional domains across grade levels. The Mindsets and Behaviors can be taught through all direct services, including classroom guidance, small group counseling, and individual counseling.

82. A: According to ASCA, mentor programs benefit students in a variety of ways. Students who participate in a mentor program and are matched with trained mentors have been shown to have increased academic outcomes across subject areas; improved attendance; reduced truancy rates; and, for African American students specifically, there is data to support a reduction in the achievement gap for students who participate in a mentor program. While there is also data to support increased homework completion and improved class participation, improved executive functioning skills are not typically a product of a mentor program.

83. D: Each of the first three options describes a typical, appropriate goal for the initial or "forming" stage of group counseling, which typically takes place in the first or second session. Conflict between group members typically develops in the transition or "storming" stage of the group. Later stages include working or "norming," and termination or "adjourning."

84. A: In this situation, Mrs. Johnson was primarily advocating for her student's legal rights under Section 504. Typically, the leadership role applies to the development and delivery of a comprehensive school counseling program, while the consultant role usually involves a third party. Convening a team meeting may involve collaboration, but the counselor's role in this scenario was as an advocate for the rights of her student.

85. C: School counselors should always follow school and district policy when students are in crisis or expressing suicidal ideation; in instances where those policies are not safe or appropriate, counselors should advocate for policies to be changed. Students who express suicidal ideation should always be taken seriously, and counselors have a duty to warn a student's parents in order to protect the student. In the situation described, Amy appears to be actively in crisis, so an immediate referral to a professional for evaluation and support is appropriate. It does not appear that Amy has time to wait for her parents to make an appointment with a therapist. Without any expression of concerns about abuse or neglect at home, Child Protective Services would not be an appropriate referral. No-harm contracts and suicide contracts are not recommended, and they place the student at risk of harm and the counselor at risk of liability.

86. C: The water glass task described in this question is a well-known demonstration of Piaget's concept of conservation. Typically, children develop the concept of conservation during the concrete operational stage (ages 7-11). Assimilation describes the process of utilizing an existing schema to understand new information, while accommodation describes changing an existing schema to understand new information. Classification is the process of grouping objects according to similar properties (such as size or color).

87. D: Kelly's symptoms could be consistent with ADHD. For a child to be diagnosed with ADHD, they must present with six or more symptoms, in at least two settings, for six months or more. Children can be diagnosed with a combined presentation (both inattentive and hyperactive-impulsive symptoms), predominantly inattentive presentation (six or more inattentive symptoms, but fewer than six hyperactive-impulsive symptoms), or predominantly hyperactive-impulsive presentation (six or more hyperactive-impulsive symptoms, but fewer than six inattentive symptoms). Since the description of Kelly's symptoms does not include any hyperactive-impulsive symptoms, it is likely that the symptoms being described align with a predominantly inattentive presentation. Task avoidance could be a symptom of generalized anxiety disorder or a specific learning disability, and forgetfulness could be an anxiety symptom. While some of the symptoms described align with the diagnoses listed in other answer choices, the six symptoms together describe a child who likely has ADHD.

88. C: Many counselors utilize online or electronic surveys for the ease of instantly collecting data from students, which can then be analyzed and disaggregated quickly without having to manually transfer data to a spreadsheet or calculate results by hand. As with all electronic communications, special consideration should be made for protecting student confidentiality, and online communications are not necessarily more confidential than other forms of communication. Answers B and D are highly dependent on the counselor's skill level with technology, the students' skill level with technology, and the format of the survey; those answer choices would not necessarily be a benefit for this type of survey.

89. C: Self-confidence in the ability to succeed is a mindset for student success, not a behavior. The mindset standards are related to attitudes and beliefs of students, whereas the behavior standards refer to demonstrated skills or actions. It is important to understand the difference between these two types of standards and how they apply to various activities when planning the comprehensive counseling program.

90. A: A reliable assessment is one that is consistent, meaning the same test-taker or group of test-takers will have similar results on the assessment when taken multiple times. Validity refers to whether or not the assessment measures what it was intended to measure. Standard deviation and stanine are both terms used to describe the distribution of scores on a standard bell curve.

91. D: Stanine measurements divide a standard bell curve into nine equal groups, and a stanine score places an individual score within one of those nine groups. A stanine score of 5 is the mean, or average, with stanine 1 being far below average and stanine 9 being far above average. Stanine scores allow an individual to interpret their score in relation to the rest of the group.

92. B: The gatekeeper of a group is the member who tries to keep everyone else on task and ensure they are participating in the group. The scapegoat is the group member whom everyone else tries to blame when things go wrong. The energizer is the group member who attempts to get others excited and enthusiastic about the group, and the interrogator asks a lot of questions of the group.

93. A: When sharing results of the school counseling program with stakeholders, counselors utilize a variety of data sources to demonstrate the impact the counseling program has on students and to advocate for their students and their role within the school. The use-of-time assessment is an important tool for school counselors, not only to evaluate their alignment with the ASCA National Model recommendation of 80% of time spent on direct and indirect service to students, but to advocate for appropriate roles within the school. The use-of-time assessment is frequently completed as part of the Manage component of an ASCA National Model program, but the Assess component is where the assessment is evaluated and areas for improvement are identified. When counselors share the results of the use-of-time assessment with school administrators, they can use the data within the analysis to support their requests for inappropriate duties to be reassigned in order to allow the counselor to achieve program goals.

94. D: Communication is not a category for the function of a behavior. While many would say that all behavior is a form of communication, the function of the behavior is what the individual is trying to accomplish with the behavior. Behavior may be an attempt to escape or avoid something unpleasant such as tasks, people, or environments; to gain or access something desirable like attention, control, or tangibles (such as toys); or for sensory input such as stimulation or regulation. Different functional behavior assessment forms may use slightly different terms (such as "avoidance" instead of "escape"), but the functions almost always fall in these categories.

95. A: The Management component of the ASCA National Model includes the use of time assessments and calendars, all of which have multiple modalities for online or electronic formats. The other answer choices all apply to the Delivery component as part of classroom guidance or individual student planning. Choice B is part of classroom guidance, which is the Delivery component, but the data collected could also be utilized in the Accountability component in reviewing the counseling program's impact on student success.

96. B: Peer mediation programs train student mediators to guide their peers through a collaborative conflict resolution process. Described as a "win-win" style, this conflict resolution style attempts to find a common solution that both parties can agree on. Other styles of conflict resolution may result in both parties not agreeing on the outcome. The competing style forces one member of the conflict to "win" at the expense of others, while the accommodating style sees one member of the conflict give in to the needs of the other member over their own. The avoiding style is exactly what it sounds like, and the conflict is ignored or postponed rather than addressed.

97. C: As with most solution-focused brief counseling, the process of termination is guided by the client's understanding of their own goal and picturing their desired outcomes. Asking the client how they will know when they are done with their counseling sessions allows the client to visualize their desired outcome and articulate the specifics of their goal. While there is not a limit to the number of sessions in this type of therapy, the number of sessions is typically limited because clients make progress quickly. Goal progress and readiness for termination are measured by the client's perception, not the counselor's observation. The client may not have completely met their goal by the time they are ready to terminate their counseling sessions, but rather may have made a great deal of progress toward that goal and feel confident in their ability to continue to make progress.

98. D: Counseling is a direct student service, while consulting, collaborating, and evaluating are all indirect services. Specifically, counseling is a responsive, direct service. Consultation and collaboration can be easily confused for direct services because they involve working directly with other professionals or stakeholders, often in "direct" response to a student need. However, direct services are defined as services provided to students.

99. A: The annual calendar is a separate document from the annual agreement. The annual agreement primarily focuses on the collaborative relationship between the counselor and principal, including the expectations for the counselor's duties, activities, use of time, and program goals. The annual agreement helps the counselor and principal both clarify priorities for the program and the desired activities to achieve those priorities.

100. B: Group leaders use blocking to stop (or "block") inappropriate or harmful behavior within the group. In this scenario, the counselor may use blocking to prevent the group member from monopolizing the conversation and then redirect the discussion to another group member.

101. C: The School Counselor Performance Appraisal is a part of the Accountability component of an ASCA National Model program. The specifics of the tools used to complete the appraisal are based on school, district, or state guidelines and processes. ASCA recommends that School Counselor Performance Appraisals include a self-evaluation component in addition to an administrative evaluation and assessment of goal attainment. Like all program evaluation tools, the School Counselor Performance Appraisal should be based on a variety of data. This tool can be utilized by the school counselor and school administrators to make program decisions and adjustments.

102. D: There are multiple factors that affect a student's educational outcomes, and students from low-socioeconomic status (SES) households are deeply affected by their circumstances. Numerous studies demonstrate the links between low-SES backgrounds and a variety of outcomes, including poor academic outcomes, lower graduation rates, inadequate literacy skills, and lower rates of college enrollment. While the home circumstances of a low-SES student affect their academic outcomes, the school environment of low-SES students is a stronger predictor of academic outcomes. Schools in low-SES communities are less likely to have highly qualified teachers with years of experience and high-quality training, as well as access to libraries and computers. All of these factors impact the academic outcomes for students in these communities, possibly even more than their home and family circumstances.

103. B: A needs assessment is a type of perception data that is commonly used to plan a comprehensive school counseling program. Needs assessments help a counselor identify areas of strength and need in their school in order to make decisions about programming. Although the school data profile is another helpful document outlining data that can be used to plan a school counseling program, it is not a type of perception data. The school data profile focuses on demographic and outcome data. Pre-test data is a type of perception data, but it wouldn't be used to plan a comprehensive school counseling program; instead, pre-test data could be used to evaluate prior knowledge of a topic or to compare to the post-test data to establish the effectiveness of an intervention. Finally, achievement testing data is a type of outcome data, and while it can be part of the planning process (for example, it is part of the school data profile), achievement testing data alone would not provide enough information to plan a comprehensive school counseling program.

104. C: In this scenario, the student is predicting that the worst possible outcome will happen as a result of their grade; in other words, they are assuming things are worse than they actually are. Personalization involves the client assuming the behaviors and reactions of others are always about them ("The teacher gave me a bad grade, so she obviously doesn't like me"). Emotional reasoning is when the client believes that if they feel a certain way, it must be true ("If I feel like a failure, I must be a failure"). Labeling involves giving a name to the situation ("I failed this test, so I am an idiot").

105. D: According to the ASCA Ethical Standards for School Counselors, counselors should avoid using personal social media accounts, email addresses, or phone numbers for any communication with parents or students. The ethical standards further encourage counselors to follow local policies and only utilize district-approved social media platforms or pages for the distribution of "vital information." In answer A, the purpose of the social media updates does fall within the ethical guidelines, but the school counselor should not utilize her personal page for these purposes.

106. B: Good grades in themselves are not necessarily a protective factor against drug use; in fact, a drop in previously high grades can be a warning sign of drug use. Intelligence and school competence can be protective factors, along with high self-esteem, strong and healthy peer groups, the ability to make friends, supportive and nurturing family relationships, temperament, and parenting styles. Protective factors can reduce the impact of risk factors for drug and alcohol abuse. Risk factors include family trauma, sexual or physical abuse, parental drug or alcohol abuse, poverty, and aggression.

107. C: The school counselor is an appropriate and often necessary member of the school-based 504 team. School counselors can advocate for their students' needs and provide valuable information about best practices for addressing the specific barriers that students with disabilities may face. Federal law requires that all 504 decisions be made by a multi-member team with a variety of knowledge, so the school counselor alone would not be able to determine eligibility and write a plan as described in answer A. Additionally, the school counselor would not be conducting assessments as described in answer B, although they may be involved in analyzing existing data or helping to identify the students' needs. While the school counselor could provide individual counseling as described in choice D, this is a service that should be available to all students and is generally not considered an appropriate accommodation to include in a 504 plan. Additionally, the statement in choice D that "participation in the 504 process is not appropriate for a school counselor" is false.

108. A: Preferential seating is a classroom accommodation that allows for a child to be seated in an area of the classroom that best addresses their needs; in this case, preferential seating may include the child sitting near the board for the best chance at seeing what is written. Extended time is a classroom accommodation, but the connection between difficulty seeing what is written on the board and providing extended time is not clear. Wearing glasses would probably help, but this does not describe a classroom accommodation, as glasses are not provided in the classroom. Cues or reminders to wear prescription glasses may be a good strategy for the student described, but only if forgetting to wear glasses is an issue. Finally, small group instruction describes an intervention or instructional strategy, not a classroom accommodation. In addition, the link between not being able to see the board and small group instruction is not very clear.

109. C: The McKinney-Vento Homeless Assistance Act includes families who are "doubled up," meaning living with other families or sharing housing due to loss of permanent housing, in the definition for "homeless." While these situations are often temporary, students who face housing insecurity often require additional support to ensure they are able to be successful in school. Once a child or family is referred to the school's McKinney-Vento liaison and qualified under that act, the liaison coordinates support as needed with other departments and staff members, including transportation, attendance, and providing information about housing programs. The student described in the scenario may need support with transportation, flexible attendance policies, or other supports, but the counselor should refer the child's case to the McKinney-Vento liaison first in order to establish a qualifying situation for those supports. Lack of stable housing is not the same as abuse or neglect.

110. C: Cognitive behavioral therapy is rooted in the belief that a client's emotional state is directly related to their beliefs or thoughts about their problems. Much of a client's time within cognitive behavioral therapy is spent challenging cognitions and changing self-talk, which in turn results in changing the client's emotional state. Don't confuse the ABC model in cognitive behavioral therapy with the ABC behavior model often used in schools when developing behavior interventions.

111. B: Developmental career theories focus on career development throughout a lifespan. While earlier theories such as the trait-factor approach focus on a single decision of the "best" job for life, developmental theories identify various stages an individual goes through in the process of their career development. Ginzberg and associates identified three stages (fantasy, tentative, and realistic), while Super identified five (growth, exploration, establishment, maintenance, and decline). Contemporary developmental career theories do not generally view an early-adulthood cut-off to the career development process.

112. A: The psychological theory of career choice, developed by John Holland, is the basis for the vast majority of approaches to career choice today. Holland's theory, known as either a psychological or personality theory, focuses on the fit between an individual's personality type and their work environment or career choice. The trait-factor approach developed by Frank Parsons is not as popular today as it once was. Developmental theories (such as those developed by Donald Super, Eli Ginzberg, and associates) and social learning theories (such as those of John Krumboltz) may be of interest to school counselors who work with children, but are not as widely used or popular as Holland's theory.

113. D: The formal operational stage typically includes children who are age 11 and older, therefore the majority of middle school students would be in this stage of development. The other stages represent ages 0-2 years (sensorimotor), 2-7 years (preoperational), and 7-11 years (concrete operational). Piaget's theory defines these four stages based on the linear development of logical concepts such as object permanence, symbolism, and conservation.

114. C: The working/norming stage of group counseling is when the majority of the "work" or counseling intervention takes place. Group members are focused on the concerns of individual members at this stage.

115. D: Each of the first three answer choices describes a topic or task that would be addressed in the group selection process. Informed consent, parent permission, and voluntary participation would all be established in the individual interview and invitation to the group. Allaying anxiety is typically addressed in the initial group meeting or "forming" stage of the group.

116. A: Typically, well-designed counseling groups have members representing homogeneous problem types, meaning all group members have the same or similar presenting problem, but heterogeneous personality group members, meaning they have a variety of personalities and behavioral patterns. This balance helps ensure that the group is effective in working together and that all participants can benefit from a common goal or skill development. Not all types of groups can be so particular about group membership. For example, the facilitator of an open support group has no control over selecting group members.

117. B: School counselor is not a section within the Assess component of the ASCA National Model. The Assess component focuses on evaluating program effectiveness through tools such as Annual Results Reports and measures of student impact, not on role descriptors. These sections are used to analyze how students are affected by the school counseling program. In contrast, school counselor refers to a role within the program, not a component or section used for assessment. Therefore, B is the correct answer.

118. A: This example most directly demonstrates the idea of "installation of hope," whereby group members can see others' successes and feel hopeful about their own prospects for growth and improvement. The concept of universality describes the understanding that what group members are experiencing is not unusual and they are not alone in their experiences. Group cohesiveness explains the sense of belonging that group members feel when working toward a common group goal. "Imparting information" could be a tricky answer choice in this scenario. Jim is sharing his experience with the group, but he is not necessarily sharing new information that they could learn from. "Installation of hope" is a better fit for this situation because the information Jim shared could inspire other group members in their progress.

119. A: According to ASCA, defining a program mission and vision statement and publicly sharing those statements with stakeholders is an activity that allows a counselor to demonstrate leadership. In writing these statements, the counselor defines the purpose and direction of the school counseling program and positions the counselor to lead the program toward that vision. Creating an advisory council is an example of collaboration, while referring students to community agencies and serving on IEP teams are examples of collaboration and advocacy.

120. D: ASCA's position statement on Safe Schools and Crisis Response indicates that the school counselor's role in a crisis is to promote school safety and advocate for the safety of students. Additionally, ASCA's guidance on response to a natural disaster recommends keeping routines as normal as possible, while limiting exposure to news and other media outlets and providing as much developmentally appropriate information as possible. Counselors should listen to student concerns, reassure them, and reaffirm their connection to safe adults.